CH

Wild Bill Hickok

Legends of the Wild West

Sitting Bull

Billy the Kid

Calamity Jane

Buffalo Bill Cody

Crazy Horse

Davy Crockett

Wyatt Earp

Geronimo

Wild Bill Hickok

Jesse James

Nat Love

Annie Oakley

Legends of the Wild West

Wild Bill Hickok

Liz Sonneborn

CHELSEA HOUSE
PUBLISHERS
An imprint of Infobase Publishing

Wild Bill Hickok

Copyright © 2010 by Infobase Publishing

Chelsea House
An imprint of Infobase Publishing
132 West 31st Street
New York NY 10001

Library of Congress Cataloging-in-Publication Data
Sonneborn, Liz.
  Wild Bill Hickok / Liz Sonneborn.
     p. cm. — (Legends of the Wild West)
  Includes bibliographical references and index.
  ISBN 978-1-60413-593-0 (hardcover)
  1. Hickok, Wild Bill, 1837–1876—Juvenile literature. 2. Peace officers—West (U.S—Biography—Juvenile literature. 3. Frontier and pioneer life—West (U.S.)—Juvenile literature. 4. West (U.S.)—Biography—Juvenile literature. 5. West (U.S.)—History—1860–1890—Juvenile literature. I. Title. II. Series.
  F594.H62S68 2010
  978'.02092—dc22
  [B]   2010006582

Text design by Kerry Casey
Cover design by Keith Trego
Composition by EJB Publishing Services
Cover printed by Bang Printing, Brainerd, Minn.
Book printed and bound by Bang Printing, Brainerd, Minn.
Date printed: July 2010
Printed in the United States of America

10 9 8 7 6 5 4 3 2 1

This book is printed on acid free paper.

CONTENTS

THE TWO WILD BILLS

In the summer of 1865, 29-year-old journalist George Ward Nichols arrived in the sleepy town of Springfield, Missouri. He was chasing a story. While serving in the Union Army during the Civil War (1861–1865), he had heard spectacular tales of a courageous sharpshooter known as Wild Bill Hickok. Nichols sensed that Hickok was the kind of character Americans everywhere were interested in reading about. Raised in Boston, Massachusetts, Nichols was sure that people in the eastern United States would be especially intrigued by Wild Bill's western adventures. Easterners in big cities, who spent their days in factories and offices, were thrilled by stories of the West, particularly exciting tales of gunslingers and outlaws battling for control over the lawless frontier.

THE JOURNALIST AND THE GUNMAN

During his stay in Springfield, Nichols met Richard Bentley Owen, a respected army captain. A friend of Hickok, Owen agreed to introduce the two men. On September 13, the young journalist

During the 1800s, lawmen and gunfighters gained notoriety through popular fiction known as dime novels. Many of the novels featured real men, but the stories were exaggerated. This cover of *Boadle's Weekly* features Buffalo Bill, Wild Bill Hickok, and Texas Jack.

and the gunman—born only one month apart—sat down for an interview.

Based on his conversation with Hickok and on interviews with other townspeople, Nichols wrote an article titled "Wild Bill." The piece ran as the cover story in the February 1867 issue of *Harper's New Monthly Magazine*. The popular national magazine had a wide readership throughout the United States. It had a smaller, though substantial, following in England as well.

As the article began, Nichols set the scene. He wrote that Springfield was filled with "strange, half-civilized people . . . dressed in queer costumes; men [wore] coats and trousers made of [animal] skin, . . . thickly covered with dirt and grease. . . . Others [wore] homespun gear, which oftentimes appeared to have seen lengthy service." The rustic town's modest shops ran down its main street. Its public square was a meeting place for "groups of men lolling against posts, lying upon the wooden sidewalks, or sitting in chairs . . . lazily occupied in doing nothing . . . their highest ambition to let their hair and beards grow."

In this lazy, slow-moving world, Hickok stood out. Recalling his first impressions of Hickok after Owen (called "Captain Honesty" in the article) introduced them, Nichols described Wild Bill as a powerful, charismatic figure:

> As I looked at him I thought his the handsomest physique I had ever seen. . . . Bill stood six feet and an inch in his bright yellow moccasins. A deer-skin shirt, or frock it might be called, hung jauntily over his shoulders, and revealed a chest whose breadth and depth were remarkable. These lungs had had growth in some twenty years of the free air of the Rocky Mountains. His small, round waist was girthed by a belt which held two of Colt's navy revolvers.

An engraving accompanied the description. It showed a tall, handsome man with hair down to his shoulders, a bushy mustache, and a wide-rimmed hat cocked to the left. The belt worn over his long coat held a holster, on which his right hand rested, ready to pull out his gun at any moment.

A MATTER OF HONOR

When Nichols began to recount Hickok's adventurous life, he started with an event that took place just a few months before Nichols came to town. The narrative was told in the words of Captain Honesty, whose account Nichols assured his readers was completely "unprejudiced." Although Captain Honesty was based on Owen, the language attributed to him was of Nichols's own creation. Owen was a sophisticated, well-spoken man. Captain Honesty, on the other hand, spoke in a folksy dialect that Easterners expected from western characters.

Captain Honesty's story began one night when Hickok was playing poker at the Lyons Hotel, while being carefully watched by a man named Davis Tutt (also known as Dave Tutt and David Tutt). "Bill had killed Dave Tutt's mate [during the war], and, a tween one thing and another, there war an unusual hard feelin' atwixt 'em," Honesty recalled. After Hickok won $200 in the game, Tutt demanded Hickok pay him $40 that Wild Bill owed him for a horse trade. Hickok gave Tutt the money.

Tutt then demanded $35 more for another debt. Hickok said, "I think yer wrong, Dave. It's only twenty-five dollars. I have a memorandum of it in my pocket down stairs. Ef its thirty-five dollars I'll give it yer." Tutt ignored Hickok's efforts to resolve the situation. Instead, he grabbed Hickok's watch, which was sitting on the table. Tutt said he would keep the watch until Hickok paid him the full $35. According to Captain Honesty, "This made Bill shooting mad; fur, don't yer see, Colonel [Nichols], it was a-doubting his honor like." Friends of Tutt's further provoked Hickok by insulting him behind his back and daring him to fight. They spread word around the town that Tutt, just to spite Hickok, was planning on carrying the watch while crossing the public square the following noon.

Captain Honesty asked Hickok if he intended to fight Tutt. "Don't you bother yerself Captain," Hickok replied. "It's not the first time I have been in a fight; and these d—d hounds have put on me long enough."

SHOOTOUT IN SPRINGFIELD

At precisely noon the next day, Hickok walked into the square. A crowd, including many of Tutt's friends, had gathered behind him. Hickok then saw Tutt standing outside the town's courthouse. Tutt walked forward into the square, with Hickok's eyes on him all the while. The two men moved toward each other until, when they were "bout fifty yards apart," Tutt pulled out his pistol. Hickok whipped his own free of its holster, and the two men fired at the same time.

Although Tutt was famous for his marksmanship, his shot sailed over Hickok's head. Tutt was not so lucky. As Captain Honesty explained, "[Hickok's] ball went through Dave's heart. He stood stock-still for a second or two, then raised his arm as if ter fire again, then he swayed a little, staggered three or four steps, and then fell dead." Hickok was so confident in his shooting skill ("Bill never shoots twice at the same man," Honesty said) that he did not even stop to see where his bullet landed before swinging around and pointing his weapon at Tutt's buddies. Then Hickok, "cool as an alligator," asked them, "Aren't yer satisfied, gentlemen? Put up your shootin-irons, or there'll be more dead men here." All the men put their guns away and agreed that "it war a far fight."

INVENTING A HERO

Today this type of shootout is familiar to nearly all Americans. Even if they have never heard Hickok's or Tutt's name, they likely know this classic scene from countless westerns—movies and television shows dealing with life in the American West during the late nineteenth century. All these shootout scenes had their origins in Nichols's description of the fight between Wild Bill Hickok and Davis Tutt.

Nichols's *Harper's* article had an even greater legacy: It introduced the world to the mythic hero known as Wild Bill Hickok. Before meeting Nichols, Hickok was known in the West as an excellent shootist and a skilled guide. But after Nichols's article appeared,

George Ward Nichols's *Harper's New Monthly Magazine* article about the exploits of Wild Bill Hickok made a star of the frontiersman. At the same time, Nichols's colorful account was considered so far fetched that it helped to end his career as a journalist of the American West. Pictured is the first published picture of Wild Bill Hickok from the February 1867 issue of *Harper's New Monthly Magazine*.

he became famous throughout the United States and beyond. Readers across America and Europe learned about the amazing Wild Bill through Nichols's article.

Nichols's account of the Hickok-Tutt gunfight was roughly accurate, although details were exaggerated and sensationalized. (For instance, Nichols hinted that the roots of the dispute between Tutt and Hickok involved a woman, which was probably untrue.) Other tales he told in the *Harper's* article were far more fanciful. For instance, much of the piece was devoted to an account of the McCanles affair. As Nichols told it, supposedly using Hickok's own words, the great gunslinger in 1861 encountered a band of bad men, led by David McCanles (also known as David M'Kandlas and David McKandles), who were determined to murder him. Single-handedly, Hickok took on the McCanles Gang. He not only killed all 10 members, but survived to tell the tale.

The story was incredible, but Nichols did his best to make a case to his readers that, in the strange world of the frontier West, anything was possible:

> As I write out the details of this terrible tale from notes which I took as the words fell from the scout's [Hickok's] lips, I am conscious of its extreme improbability; but while I listened to him I remembered the story in the Bible, where we are told that Samson with the jawbone of an ass slew a thousand men, and as I looked upon this magnificent example of human strength and daring, he appeared to me to realize the powers of a Samson and Hercules combined, and I should not have been inclined to place any limit on his achievements.

A MAN AND A LEGEND

Not all readers were as easily convinced. Many reporters, especially in the West, complained that Nichols's stories were way too far-fetched to be true. No newspaper was more dismissive than Springfield's. As the first copies of Nichols's article reached the town, the

Springfield Weekly Patriot reported that "some [townspeople] are excessively indignant, but the great majority are in convulsions of laughter." The paper maintained that Nichols had spent most of his time in Springfield in saloons, "seriously endangering the supply of lager and corn whisky, and putting on more airs than a spotted stud-horse in the ring of a county fair."

The *Patriot* did not blame Hickok, whom it called "a remarkable man," for Nichols's outlandish claims. It instead assumed that Hickok was appalled by what had been written about him: "In reading the romantic and pathetic parts of the article, . . . we tried to fancy Bill's familiar face while listening to the passage being read. We could almost hear his certain remark, 'O! hell! what a d—n fool that Nichols is.' We agree with 'Wild Bill' on that point."

The criticism helped end Nichols's career as a journalist of the American West. Although he continued to write for *Harper's* on a variety of topics, he eventually settled in Cincinnati, Ohio, where he devoted himself to articles and books about safer subjects, such as music, art education, and pottery.

Other writers, however, were only too eager to capitalize on the popular western character Nichols had created. Accounts of Hickok and his exploits became a central part of the burgeoning industry of novels and other writings about the "Wild West." As a result, the story of Wild Bill Hickok has ever since been a tale of two men—a real person named James Butler Hickok and the mythic hero that, for him, proved to be both a boon and a burden.

THIRSTING FOR ADVENTURE

James Butler Hickok, who later became known as Wild Bill, was born on May 27, 1837, in Illinois. His parents, William and Polly, had moved there from New York State four years earlier. James was the youngest of their four sons. In addition to his brothers Oliver, Lorenzo, and Horace, his parents would later welcome two daughters—Celinda and Lydia—into the household.

Hickok's first ancestor to arrive in North America was on his mother's side. He was a Dutchman named Thomas Blossom, who arrived in the colony of Massachusetts in 1629. (Two U.S. presidents—George W. Bush and Barack Obama—can also trace their ancestry back to Blossom. They are, therefore, very distantly related to Wild Bill Hickok.) Six years later, Englishman William Hickocks, an ancestor on his father's side, also came to Massachusetts. By the time the United States won its independence from England in 1783, descendants of William Hickocks were living all over New England. James's father grew up in Vermont, but like many men of his generation, as an adult he headed west in search of better financial opportunities.

Only a few years before the Hickok family arrived in northern Illinois, the area was embroiled in a vicious conflict between Sac and Fox Indians and non-Indian settlers who were taking over their land. In 1832, the American Indians were defeated in what became known as Black Hawk's War. With Indian attacks no longer a threat, white farmers moved quickly to claim plots in the Sac and Fox's former homeland.

A BOY IN ILLINOIS

Joining the land rush, William Hickok settled in Homer, Illinois, which was later renamed Troy Grove when it was discovered that there was already another Illinois town called Homer. For a time, William made a good living in Troy Grove as a storekeeper. But during the year James was born, the United States suffered a

Pictured is the house where Hickok was born in Troy Grove, Illinois. His father's farm was used as one of the "stations" or safe houses on the Underground Railroad.

severe economic downturn. William lost his business, and for years he struggled to keep his family fed by working odd jobs at nearby farms. With the help of his older sons, he was able to establish his own small farm by the early 1850s.

Throughout James's boyhood, William Hickok was an abolitionist—a person who opposed the practice of slavery and wanted it abolished (ended) in the United States. He did more than just speak out against slavery. He was also actively involved in the Underground Railroad, a network of safe houses where runaway slaves could spend a night as they fled north to freedom. Runaways sometimes stayed in the Hickok family home, possibly in a hidden cellar that William Hickok built just for this purpose. According to family lore, young James and his father once aided fleeing slaves as they were being chased by a pack of armed bounty hunters.

As a boy, James's day-to-day life was hardly so dramatic. He spent much of his time hunting, a valuable skill for a young man wanting to put meat on his large family's dinner table. In Troy Grove, James gained a reputation as a talented marksman, but even as a young teenager he longed for something more. In 1851, when his brother Oliver left home to prospect for gold in California, James desperately wanted to go with him. His father said he was too young, and besides he was needed at home. That same year, when his father was on a trip, he wrote a letter to James and his older brother Horace to remind them both of their family responsibilities: "James, I shall hope to have a good acount [sic] of you when I get home. Horace, I depend much upon you in my absence [and I] hope you and James will be friendly & steady & stay at home as much as possible & do all you can for your Mother & be kind to the Girls."

After William Hickok died in 1852, the family left the farm and moved to town. The new situation only made James more restless. Hickok biographer Joseph G. Rosa suggests that James's domineering mother may have been difficult to live with. With his father no longer there to mediate between them, James may have bristled at her demands, fueling even more his desire to escape his childhood home.

Early Western Heroes

Long before Wild Bill Hickok became a legend in his own time, Americans were building myths about famous frontiersmen living on the nation's western border. In fact, when Hickok was a boy, several real western adventurers had already been turned into famous legendary characters celebrated across the United States.

Daniel Boone (1734–1820)

Born in Pennsylvania, Boone was an early explorer of what is now Kentucky, which in the late eighteenth century was largely a wilderness area. In 1775, after marking a trail between present-day Virginia and Kentucky known as the Wilderness Road, Boone bought a tract of land from the Cherokee Indians on which he established a settlement he called Boonesborough. Having opened Kentucky to non-Indian settlement, he later led a group of white settlers into what is now Missouri. Boone's bold trailblazing inspired a series of authors to write books mythologizing his achievements. The most popular was Timothy Flint's *Biographical Memoir of Daniel Boone* (1834), which was one of the most widely read books in early nineteenth century America. In that book and other accounts, Boone was hailed both as a simple man of action and as a needed agent of civilization who tamed the wilderness for settlers destined to follow him west.

Davy Crockett (1786–1836)

A native of Tennessee, Davy Crockett first made a name for himself in the military before embarking on a political career. He served both in the Tennessee state legislature (1821–1824) and in the U.S. Congress (1827–

LIVING IN KANSAS TERRITORY

In 1856, when James was 19, he finally got his chance. The U.S. government had recently opened up Kansas Territory for non-Indian settlement. The Hickok family decided that James and his brother

1831, 1833–1835). Crockett and his supporters created an image of him as a fearless frontiersman capable of superhuman acts of daring, including battling bears in hand-to-hand combat. His myth only grew after he was killed at the Alamo during Texas's war for independence from Mexico in 1836. The legendary Crockett later became the subject of plays, songs, novels, and movies. The Crockett character proved so durable that he became a television phenomenon more than a hundred years after Crockett's death. In the 1950s, a hit television series about Crockett, produced by Walt Disney, was extremely popular and sparked a national craze. Children everywhere wore hats made out of fake raccoon skin in imitation of their television hero.

Kit Carson (1809–1868)

As a teenager, Christopher "Kit" Carson ran away from his home in present-day Missouri and headed west to what is now New Mexico. In the West, he found work as a teamster (stagecoach driver) and as an animal trapper. In 1842, he met John C. Frémont, who hired him as a guide for a series of expeditions into what are now California and Oregon. Carson later served in the military during the Mexican-American War (1846–1848) and the Civil War (1861–1865), rising to the rank of brigadier general. As early as 1849, Carson emerged as a larger than life character in western fiction. Wild Bill Hickok himself seemed taken with the heroics attributed to Carson. According to his sister Lydia, as a young man Hickok boasted that he would someday have adventures Kit Carson "never thought of doing." Carson's myth was furthered after his death by his representation in *Memoirs of My Life* (1886) by Frémont, who, with the help of his wife Jessie, displayed a keen gift for promoting himself and his friends.

Lorenzo should strike out for this western region and claim land there. If they were successful in establishing a farm, the rest of the family would follow them.

By the summer, James and Lorenzo were in Kansas. Soon, they received word that their mother was ill. (Hickok's biographer, Rosa, suggests that Polly Hickok might have been pretending to be sick to force her boys to return home.) Lorenzo decided to head back to Illinois, but James elected to stay put.

However, James discovered that Kansas was hardly a peaceful place to establish a homestead. It was almost a battlefield. Like Hickok, most Kansans were against slavery. However, the citizens of the neighboring state of Missouri, where slavery was legal, were mostly for slavery. Missourian slave owners feared that, if Kansas Territory outlawed slavery, their slaves would try to escape over the border. To make matters even more complicated, when the Kansas-Nebraska Act of 1854 created the territories of Kansas and Nebraska, it required settlers in those territories to vote on whether they would allow slavery within their borders. Determined to vote for slavery in Kansas, Missourians flooded into the territory. The tensions between the pro-slavery and antislavery factions quickly erupted into violence, which lasted from 1854 to 1858. Federal troops had to rush to Kansas to keep these two groups from slaughtering each other. Hickok may have joined the conflict on the side of the antislavery Kansans. In a letter home, he wrote that "thare is 29 of our company in custody at Lacompton [Lecompton]," which suggests that he was part of an armed antislavery group that had had a run-in with U.S. soldiers.

Hickok had originally settled in Leavenworth County, Kansas Territory. But late in 1856, he was befriended by an Englishman named Robert H. Williams, who persuaded him to join a southward expedition to the recently established Johnson County. By early 1858, Hickok was living there in the village of Monticello. In March, Monticello held its first election. At only 20 years old, Hickok became one of four constables elected by the village. In this position, Hickok had his first experience in law enforcement.

For the most part, being a constable meant delivering summonses and tracking down horse thieves. But a letter home, which Hickok probably wrote during the time he lived in Monticello, suggests he also had to deal with some degree of frontier violence: "[Y]ou don [k]now what a Country this is for drinking and fighting but I hope it will be different some time. . . . Thare has been

In 1858, at just 20 years old, Hickok was elected as a constable in Monticel-lo, Kansas. He was charged with delivering summonses, tracking down horse thieves, and stopping various acts of violence. Here he is pictured at the age of 21.

two awful fights in town this week you don't know anything about sutch [*sic*] fighting at home as I speak of this is no place for women and children yet."

Hickok himself, however, was not above sampling the saloons and gambling parlors of Kansas. His mother expressed concern that her youngest son was drinking too much. Hickok jokingly wrote to one of his brothers that he was going to tell him some lies and then said everything his mother wanted to hear—that he had quit drinking, chewing tobacco, and flirting with women.

In 1859, Hickok left Monticello and began working on a nearby farmed owned by John M. Owen. There, he became acquainted with Owen's daughter Mary Jane. Hickok sent a letter home with a lock of his hair, which, he explained, Mary Jane had snipped off for him. Hickok's mother rightly guessed that James and Mary Jane were romantically involved and sent Lorenzo to Kansas to persuade James to end the relationship. Mary Jane was part Shawnee Indian, and the Hickoks, like many white Americans of the day, were prejudiced against American Indians. Lorenzo succeeded in his mission. Soon after his brother arrived, James returned to Leavenworth County and Mary Jane married another man.

TROUBLE AT ROCK CREEK

Not much is recorded about Hickok's life over the next two years, but most accounts maintain that he and his brother Lorenzo worked for the Russell, Majors, and Waddell overland stage company. With its headquarters in the town of Leavenworth, this large freighting company carried supplies for the U.S. military and other clients. Hickok likely worked as a teamster—a driver of a stagecoach or a wagon pulled by a team of horses. He probably carried goods on the Santa Fe Trail, which connected Missouri to the trading center at what is now Santa Fe, New Mexico.

In the spring of 1861, Hickok arrived in the town of Rock Creek in Nebraska Territory. He was most likely still employed by Russell, Majors, and Waddell. Because of an injury (possibly the result of a fight with a bear), he was sidelined into a less physically demanding job than driving coaches. At Rock Creek, there was a relay station operated by the freighting firm. Hickok was hired to take care of the horses and mules the company kept there.

Also stationed at Rock Creek was Horace Wellman. Living there with his wife, Jane, he was the superintendent at the station.

Soon after starting the job, Wellman was confronted by a very angry man named David McCanles. Once the sheriff of Watauga County in North Carolina, McCanles had moved to Nebraska Territory and bought the station building at Rock Creek. Some accounts say he left North Carolina to escape creditors and to desert his wife and children, but records show his family soon joined him in Rock Creek. After building a successful toll bridge and establishing a ranch, McCanles sold the station building to Russell, Majors, and Waddell in April 1861. The company paid him one-third of the purchase price upfront and promised to give him the rest in two installments, one in June and one in July. But to McCanles's fury, the company reneged on the deal. When he received neither the June nor the July payment, he took his grievance to Wellman. McCanles said Wellman needed to get him his money or vacate the station.

Trying to calm McCanles, Wellman agreed to look into the matter. He traveled to Brownville, where the company's regional office was located, to discuss the problem with his supervisor. McCanles's 12-year-old son, Monroe, went along on the trip. While they were away, McCanles went to the station several times to demand his money, sometimes directing his anger at Hickok. McCanles also had a fistfight with Jane Wellman's father, whom McCanles accused of stealing a horse and wagon.

Wellman returned to Rock Creek on July 12, 1861. That afternoon, McCanles with Monroe, cousin James Woods, and employee James Gordon headed to Wellman's house to hear his report from Brownville. The news was not good. Russell, Majors, and Waddell was in financial trouble. Wellman had no idea when McCanles would see his money. He also claimed he did not have the authority to return the station to McCanles.

A DISAGREEMENT TURNS VIOLENT

What happened next is still open to question. Retellings of the event vary wildly. But most likely Wellman ended the conversation and

An Eyewitness Account of the Rock Creek Incident

In 1927, *Nebraska History* magazine devoted an entire issue to the 1861 incident at Rock Creek, in which three men were murdered, possibly at the hand of Wild Bill Hickok. The issue included an article titled "The Only Living Eye Witness," which featured a letter from 77-year-old Monroe Mc-Canles, the son of David McCanles, one of the men who had died at Rock Creek. In the letter, he gave his own version of the shootings, which he had witnessed when he was 12:

> [My father] stepped up on the step [outside the Wellman house] and said, "Now, Jim [Wild Bill Hickok], if you have anything against me, come out and fight me fair." Just as he uttered these words the gun cracked and he fell flat on his back. He raised himself up to almost a sitting position and took one last look at me, then fell back dead.
>
> Now Woods and Gordon heard the shout and came running up unarmed to the door, and just then Jim appeared at the door with a Colt's navy revolver. He fired two shots at Woods, and Woods ran around the house to the north. Gordon broke and ran. Jim ran out of the door and fired two shots at him and wounded him. Just as Jim ran out of the door Wellman came out with a hoe and ran after Woods who had run around the house, and hit Woods on the head

went inside. His wife then started yelling at McCanles, and Hickok, who was in the house, came to the door. McCanles demanded he come outside, but Hickok remained where he was. McCanles then went to another door, possibly hoping to attract Wellman's attention, and asked Hickok for a drink of water.

Suddenly, a shot rang out. McCanles's body fell to the ground. His son Monroe ran over to McCanles, but Jane Wellman chased with a hoe and finished him. Then Wellman came running around the house where I was standing and struck at me with the hoe and he yelled out "let's kill them all." I dodged the lick and ran. I outran him to a ravine shelter south of the house and stopped there. Mrs. Wellman stood in the door clapping her hands and yelling "kill him, kill him, kill him." . . .

Gordon kept a blood hound that usually followed him where he went. . . . After Gordon had made his getaway, being wounded, the station outfit put this dog on his trail. . . . When the bunch caught up, the dog was fighting Gordon, and Gordon was warding him off with a stick. Gordon was finished with a load of buck shot. . . .

When I made my escape from Wellman I ran three miles to the ranch and broke the news to my mother. One of our hands hitched up a team and took mother and the other children up to the Station. I was so exhausted with my getaway that I remained at the ranch, or home place. . . . After the killing, my uncle, J.L. McCanles, organized a crowd over in Johnson county and came over and arrested Hick-ok, Wellman and Dock [*sic*] Brink and took them before a Justice of the Peace at Beatrice, Nebraska, . . . and [they] were acquitted. The county was not organized at that time and the trials were crude, merely sham trials. . . .

My father was no killer, horse thief, desperado, nor anything of the kind. We trace the family back to 1770 and there have never been any of our ancestors found hanging on a limb, so far.

him away. Woods and Gordon, who were by the corral near the house, also rushed toward McCanles. In the chaos, both of them were shot. As Woods tried to escape the bullet fire, he fell down. Either Horace or Jane Wellman then grabbed a hoe and used it to beat Woods to death. Gordon managed to escape into some nearby brush, but Hickok, Wellman, and a station hand named J.W. "Doc" Brink followed him. Gordon's hunting dog chased after his master

According to some reports, David McCanles had a long-standing feud with Hickok, traceable either to Hickok's dating McCanles's girlfriend or to McCanles supposedly being the town bully. Tensions finally reached the boiling point the day McCanles came to collect a debt from Hickok's boss. McCanles was fatally shot, becoming the first man Hickok was reputed to have killed during a fight.

and gave away his location. As Gordon begged for his life, a shotgun blast killed him. Only Monroe managed to escape with his life. He ran home and told his mother what had happened.

McCanles's relatives swore out a complaint against Hickok, Wellman, and Doc Brink, accusing them of cold-blooded murder. They were arrested and taken to the town of Beatrice. There they appeared before T.M. Coulter, a justice of the peace. Hickok and his fellow defendants claimed they had acted in self-defense and in defense of their company's property. Coulter then heard the testimony of Jane Wellman, who backed up the accused. The justice, however, refused to allow young Monroe McCanles, who had witnessed all the shootings, to testify. After this hasty trial, Coulter accepted Hickok, Wellman, and Brink's defense and found that they were not guilty of any wrongdoing.

It is still unclear who fired the shots that killed McCanles, Woods, and Gordon. In many accounts, Hickok is named as the gunman, although some suggest that Wellman killed McCanles and Doc Brink shot Gordon. It is also uncertain whether McCanles and his companions were armed or not, although it seems unlikely they would not have returned fire if they had been carrying guns. McCanles was later depicted by some as, at best, a bully and, at worst, a murderous thug. But if he had come to Wellman's house looking to shed some blood, it is hard to believe he would bring his young son in tow. Whatever happened that day, a whitewashed version of the McCanles murders would soon become a central part of Hickok's legend.

THE WAR YEARS

Soon after the incident at Rock Creek, James Butler Hickok found a new employer—the army of the United States, also known as the Union Army. The nation was then embroiled in the Civil War (1861–1865). The conflict pitted states in the North against states in the South that wanted to break away from the United States and establish a new country, the Confederate States of America. The fighting force of the Southern states was called the Confederate Army.

Although Hickok worked for the Union Army, he was never a soldier. He instead was a civilian employee who largely stayed away from the battlefield. Hickok probably was first hired by the Union Army in August 1861. Few records of Hickok's war service exist, but one document does show that by October he was working in Missouri as a wagon master, a job that entailed transporting supplies. By the following September, he was no longer on the army's employment rolls.

BECOMING WILD BILL

In 1867, journalist Henry M. Stanley claimed that Hickok had been a member of the Missouri state militia during the war. Supposedly, he acted as a spy and spent months behind Confederate lines. There is no record of Hickok's militia service, but in the 1930s, a man named Alfred Block claimed he had encountered Hickok while serving in the militia. According to Block:

> [Hickok] rode past on a mule. The man was dirty & unshaven, his clothing was dirty & needed repairs, so a young recruit made some disparaging remarks to the man about his appearance. The man made no answer but looked the young fellow over as tho he wanted to remember him. After the man was out of hearing, one of the cavalrymen said: "Young fellow, you're lucky to be alive. That man you smarted off is Wild Bill Hickok, one of our scouts & he doesn't take that kind of talk from anybody."

Block may have embellished his story, but James Butler Hickok probably became "Wild Bill" sometime during the war. He was already known as "Dutch Bill" at least since 1856, when he used that name on some documents. Many years later, however, a fellow wagon master, George W. Hance, claimed that Hickok earned the "Wild Bill" nickname in 1862 when he came to rescue a bartender who was attacked by a mob. As Hickok fought off the man's enemies, an eyewitness

When Hickok was 24 years old, the Civil War broke out. He worked for the Union Army as a teamster, a wagon master, and, possibly, a spy. In this picture, Hickok is 26 years old.

supposedly yelled out, "My God, ain't he wild!" Hance called his own story into question by later offering a completely different origin of the nickname. According to Hance's second story, Hickok became known as "Wild Bill" to distinguish him from his brother Lorenzo, also a Union wagon master, who was called "Tame Bill." Regardless which story, if either, is true, the first published reference to Wild Bill Hickok dates from July 1865, so the nickname most likely dates from the Civil War years.

Although records of Hickok's service are spotty, army documents indicate that he was hired as a special policeman in Springfield, Missouri, in March 1864. By the next month, he was serving as an army scout under Captain Richard Bentley Owen in Missouri. Correspondence between Hickok and Brigadier General John B. Sanborn also shows that, by the following February, Hickok was charged with determining the number and movements of Confederate soldiers in northern Arkansas and southern Missouri. In one letter, Hickok noted, "There are not more than ten or twelve rebels [Confederates] in any squad in the southwest that I can hear of." By this time, the Confederate Army was clearly losing the war. As each day passed, more and more Confederate soldiers were deserting, as their army suffered severe shortages of food and other necessary supplies. The Confederates surrendered on April 9, 1865, and within days the news had reached Missouri that the war was over.

KILLING DAVIS TUTT

The end of the war was also the end of Hickok's job. By July, he found himself unemployed. Hickok then moved to Springfield, Missouri, where he began working for the soldiers at Springfield's fort. Hickok was supposedly responsible for ferreting out former Confederate soldiers who refused to give up the fight. According to one soldier at the fort, Hickok discovered a house where a group of Confederates were holed up. After U.S. troops had surrounded the house, Hickok knocked on the door: "They asked who was there, and he said Wild Bill. One of them swore that Wild Bill had better git [*sic*] out of there. But Bill laughed, and told them that the house was surrounded by soldiers, that they had better come out without any trouble, as we had come after them, and would git them, trouble or no trouble." The men came outside, and Hickok took all of them into custody except for one man who managed to escape. He then hunted down the runaway and turned him over to the authorities at the fort.

In Springfield, Hickok also resumed his old favorite pastime— gambling. An argument that began over a poker table led to the famous shootout in the town square, in which Hickok killed his former friend Davis Tutt. Some local newspaper reports, hoping to sensationalize the already sensational story, hinted that the two men were really fighting over a woman. But according to Major Albert Barnitz, the fort's commanding officer, the beef between Hickok and Tutt was simply a petty gambling dispute that turned very ugly. In a diary entry for July 21, 1865, Barnitz wrote:

> I had "Wild Bill" arrested at once, and turned him over to the civil authorities for trial. He is a noted scout, desperado and gambler, as was also the man who was killed. Both have been in the habit of appearing on the streets with two revolvers strapped on their belts. Both have been intimate for years and have been gambling together to-day. The ill will seems to have originated at the gambling table.

The next day, Hickok was released from jail pending his trial for murder. His bail was paid by his friend Captain Owen. Hickok's fate was hotly debated on the streets of Springfield. According to Barnitz, "Public sympathy seems about equally divided between him and his victim." One local newspaper editor took Tutt's side. He wrote that "the defendant engaged in the fight willingly," so Hickok was "not entitled to an acquit[t]al on the ground of self-defense."

Behind Enemy Lines

In his 1867 article about Wild Bill Hickok in *Harper's New Monthly Magazine,* journalist George Ward Nichols recorded several stories about Hickok's tenure as a scout for the U.S. Army during the Civil War. Although the tales were probably untrue, they became one of the most exciting parts of Hickok's legend, especially to men who had themselves fought in the war. At the beginning of this excerpt, told in Hickok's voice, he is spying behind enemy lines and puts into action a daring plan to escape and return to his regiment.

We had a big sergeant in our company [the Confederate company Hickok had infiltrated] who was alms a-braggin that he could stump any man in the regiment. He swore he had killed more Yanks [Union soldiers] than any man in the army, and that he could do more daring things than any others. So one day when he was talking loud I took him up, and offered to bet horse for horse that I would ride out into the open, and nearer to the Yankees than he. He tried to back out of this, but the men raised a row, calling him a funk, and a bragger, and all that; so he had to go. Well, we mounted our horses, but before we came within shootin' distance of the Union soldiers I made my horse kick and rear so that they could see who I was. Then we rode slowly to the river bank, side by side.

There must have been ten thousand men watching us; for, besides the rebs [Confederate soldiers] who wouldn't have cried about

TRIED FOR MANSLAUGHTER

Hickok's trial took place on August 5 and 6. By then, the charge was reduced from murder to manslaughter. During the trial, eight men gave testimony before coroner J.F. Brown. One witness, Eli J. Armstrong, said that on the day of the shootout he came upon Hickok, it if we had both been killed, our boys saw something was up, and without being seen thousands of them came down to the river. Their pickets kept firing at the sergeant; but whether or not they were afraid of putting a ball through me I don't know, but nary a shot hit him. He was a plucky feller all the same, for the bullets zitted about in every direction.

Bime-by we got right close ter the river, when one of the Yankee soldiers yelled out, "Bully for Wild Bill."

Then the sergeant suspicioned [suspected] me, for he turned on me and growled out, "By God, I believe yer a Yank!" And he at onst [once] drew his revolver; but he was too late, for the minute he drew his pistol I put a ball through him. I mightn't have killed him if he hadn't suspicioned me. I had to do it then.

As he rolled out of the saddle I took his horse by the bit, and dashed into the water as quick as I could. . . . It was the hottest bath I ever took. Whew! For about two minutes how the bullets zitted and skipped on the water. I thought I was hit again and again, but the reb sharp-shooters were bothered by the splash we made, and in a little while our boys drove them to cover, and after some tumbling at the bank got into the brush with my two horses without a scratch.

"It is a fact," said the scout, while he caressed his long hair, "I felt sort of proud when the boys took me into camp, and General Curtis thanked me before a heap of generals."

Tutt, and a third man sitting on the porch of Lyon House. After asking them what was going on, Armstrong heard both Hickok's and Tutt's stories of their dispute.

Armstrong urged Tutt to stop making trouble. He claimed in court that both men had tried to settle the argument peacefully:

"ARE YOU SATISFIED?"

In 1865, Hickok was involved in another shootout, this time with former friend Davis Tutt. After an argument during a poker game, the men faced off in the town square and Tutt was killed. One of the better known gunfights of the Old West, the Hickok-Tutt fight provided the model for shootouts in many Hollywood western films.

Haycock [Hickok] remarked to Tutt that he would rather have a fuss with any man on earth than him for you have accommodated me more than any man in town for I have borrowed money from you time and again, and we have never had any dispute before in our settlement. Tutt said he knew that & did not want any difficulty himself.

But minutes later, Tutt was in the public square, proudly displaying the watch he had swiped from Hickok—the very thing Hickok had specifically warned him not to do. Witnesses agree that, as the men faced each other, Tutt moved to pull out his gun. They disagreed about how many shots were fired. Some heard just one, which suggested that only Hickok had managed to pull the trigger.

The court instructed the six jury members to acquit Hickok if they believed Tutt had drawn his pistol and if they felt "the conduct of Tutt on this occasion with his general character known to the Deft [defendant] was such as to reasonably cause the Deft to apprehend a design on the part of Tutt to do the Deft some great personal injury." Probably in an attempt to sway the members of the jury in Hickok's favor, the instructions also reminded the jury that "when danger is threatened and impending a man is not compelled to stand with his arms folded until it is too late to offer successful resistance."

The jury found Hickok not guilty. The decision was controversial in Springfield, where many people claimed the trial was rigged. Certainly the fact that two of the jury members were former army officers who were friendly with Hickok called the jury's objectivity into question.

The town's mixed feelings about the verdict probably played a role in the outcome of its September elections, in which Hickok ran for marshal. He had enough friends and supporters to place second in a field of five candidates, but he also had enough detractors to keep him from winning the election.

The same month, journalist George Ward Nichols arrived in town. He came to Springfield with one goal in mind—to interview Wild Bill Hickok. During his distinguished service in the Civil War, Nichols had heard tales of Wild Bill's exploits. His journalistic instincts told him that Hickok would be the perfect subject for a colorful profile of a western adventurer. At Nichols's urging, Hickok's friend Captain Owen arranged a meeting between the two men. Soon after, Nichols left Springfield with thorough notes about his visit, a photograph of Hickok, and permission from Hickok to write a piece about him. Sixteen months would pass before Nichols's article appeared in print. After it did, Hickok's life would never be the same again.

BECOMING FAMOUS

By January 1866, Wild Bill Hickok was tired of Springfield, Missouri. He was happy to accept a job offer from his old friend, Captain Owen, who had been restationed at Fort Riley in Kansas. In addition to the lure of regular pay, Hickok probably looked forward to a reunion with his brother Lorenzo, who was working at the fort at the time.

At Fort Riley, Hickok became a guide and scout for the army. Throughout the next year, he went on a series of military expeditions, one of which was headed by the Civil War hero General William Tecumseh Sherman. He also worked as a guide for Colonel James F. Meline, who recorded his impressions of Hickok in his book *Two Thousand Miles on Horseback: Santa Fe and Back* (1868): "By the way, I forgot to tell you about our guide—the most striking object in camp. Six feet, lithe, active, sinewy, daring rider, dead shot with pistol and rifle, long locks, fine features and mustasche, buckskin leggins, red shirt, broad-brim hat, two pistols in belt, rifle in hand—he is a picture." Like many people who encountered Hickok, Meline also noted his delight in telling tall tales about himself: "He goes by the name of Wild Bill, and tells wonderful stories of his horsemanship, fighting, and hair-breadth escapes. We do not, however, feel under any obligation to believe them all."

Before the Civil War, Fort Riley was established to protect pioneers as they traveled west over the Oregon and Santa Fe trails. After the war, it was a common site for skirmishes between Native Americans and the U.S. Army. Here, Hickok served as a scout during the army's wars with the Plains Indians.

MEETING CUSTER

While Hickok was at Fort Riley, a brash, young lieutenant colonel named George Armstrong Custer took command of the outpost. Custer became friendly with Hickok, as did Custer's wife, Elizabeth. Clearly enamored by the handsome scout, she later wrote a glowing description of Hickok in her book *Following the Guidon* (1890):

> Physically, he was a delight to look upon. Tall, lithe and free in every motion, he rose and walked as if every muscle was perfection. . . . He was rather fantastically clad, of course, but all that seemed perfectly in keeping with the time and the place. He did not make an armoury of his waist, but carried two pistols. He wore top-boots, riding breeches, and dark blue flannel shirt, with scarlet set-in

front. A loose neck-hankerchief left his fine, firm throat free.

At the fort, Hickok also renewed his acquaintance with John "Captain Jack" Harvey, whom he had known during the war. The two became partners, following a common practice of professional scouts working in pairs. The partnership, however, soon ended with Harvey's death from tuberculosis in the spring of 1868.

Some accounts of Hickok's life say that he served as a deputy U.S. marshal at Fort Riley, but no evidence for this claim exists. For a time, however, Owen did hire Hickok as a government detective. His job was to search out and apprehend anyone caught stealing property that belonged to the U.S. government. The work mostly entailed rounding up thieves who had stolen mules and horses from the fort or who were cutting timber for sale on lands owned by the government.

A NATIONAL CELEBRITY

As 1867 began, Hickok was a familiar figure in Missouri and Kansas. Just a few weeks later, virtually overnight, he became a nationally known celebrity. The event that transformed Hickok's life was the publication of George Ward Nichols's article "Wild Bill" in the February 1867 issue of *Harper's New Monthly Magazine*. The issue quickly sold out. Nichols had guessed right: Readers all over the country were thirsty to learn about Hickok and his exciting exploits.

Newspapers in the eastern United States largely took Nichols's descriptions of Hickok's adventures at face value, without questioning how much was based on fact and how much was invented by the journalist himself. The *New York Daily Tribune*, for instance, wrote that the "whole narrative affords a rich illustration of the romance of border life." Western papers, however, generally viewed Nichols's account with a more critical eye. Those published in Hickok's old stomping grounds were particularly skeptical about Nichols's fantastic claims about his hero.

Formerly called "Duck Bill" due to his long nose and protruding lip, Hickok later became known as an impressive figure. Six foot one with perfumed, blond hair worn down to his shoulders, he often wore a black frock coat, starched collar, white shirt, scarlet vest, and boots made of calf. Journalist Henry Stanley once wrote that Hickok "is as handsome a specimen of a man as could be found."

Some critical reviews of the article complained that Hickok was not that different from other frontiersmen. They asked why Hickok had been singled out for so much laudatory attention when many other men had had similar experiences in the West. One such article appeared in the *Atchison Daily Champion*, published in Atchison, Kansas, on February 1:

> Bill was formerly a driver on the Overland Stage Line, and is well known to many old residents of this city. Few, however, would recognize him in the romantic picture Nichols draws. He was simply a desperado, and dozens like him can be found among the employees of the O.S. Line.

In a similar vein, the editor of the *Leavenworth Daily Conservative* wrote, "The story of 'Wild Bill,' as told in *Harper's* for February is not easily credited hereabouts. There are many of the rough riders of the rebellion [Civil War] now in this city whose records would compare very favorably with that of 'Wild Bill.'"

The *Missouri Weekly Patriot*'s review was particularly negative. Much of its criticism of Nichols's article, however, focused on its description of Springfield. In truth, Nichols was fairly unkind to the town. Probably wanting to paint a picture of a quaint western town that eastern readers would enjoy, he insulted the townspeople by depicting them all as lazy do-nothings. The *Patriot*, in its defense of the citizens of Springfield, suggested that Nichols could hardly be trusted, given that he had spent only a few days in the town. It also noted the obvious exaggerations and mistakes in the piece. It questioned Nichols's claims that Hickok had killed hundreds of Confederate soldiers during the war and pointedly referred to Hickok as "James B. Hickok" to mock the fact that Nichols even got his subject's real name wrong. (Nichols called him "William Hickok.")

REVISITING ROCK CREEK

In critical examinations of the *Harper's* article, Nichols's description of the Rock Creek incident frequently came under attack. Although what happened there is still not entirely clear, the account in the article is pure fiction. Supposedly quoting Hickok, Nichols called McCanles "the Captain of a gang of desperadoes, horse-thieves, murderers, regular cut-throats, who were the terror of every body on the [Kansas-Missouri] border." According to Nichols's story, Hickok was working as a guide for the army when, in 1861, he went to visit "an old friend of mine, a Mrs. Wellman." She greeted him in a panic: "Is that you, Bill? Oh, my God! They will kill you! Run! Run! They will kill you!" McCanles and his vicious gang supposedly were out to get Hickok because he had beaten McCanles at a shooting match. Holing up in the Wellman house, Hickok prepared to take on the entire band of outlaws with a revolver and a small amount of ammunition.

McCanles led the charge, but Hickok succeeded in killing him with a single shot to the heart. Then, talking to himself, he said, "Only six shots and nine men to kill. Save your powder, Bill, for the death-hugs a comin!" Even with the odds against him, the gang was no match for Hickok: "One—two—three—four; and four men fell dead." Nichols's Wild Bill then described how he dispatched with the others:

> That didn't stop the rest. Two of them fired their bird-guns at me. And then I felt a sting run all over me. The room was full of smoke. Two got in close to me, their eyes glaring out of the clouds. One I knocked down with my fist. "You are out of the way for a while," I thought. The second I shot dead. The other three clutched me and crowded me onto the bed. I fought hard. I broke with my hand one man's arm. He had his fingers round my throat. Before I could get to my feet I was struck across the breast with the stock of a rifle, and I felt the blood rushing out of my nose and mouth. Then I got ugly, and I remember that I got hold of a knife, and then it was all cloudy like, and I was wild, and I struck savage blows, following the devils up from one side to the other of the room and into the corners, striking and slashing until I knew that every one was dead.

Not surprisingly, Nichols was taken to task for such an outlandish story, which bore little resemblance to any report of the incident. The *Atchison Daily Champion*, for instance, pointed out that
the "McKandles [McCanles] gang consisted of only the leader and
three others, and not of fourteen as stated in the magazine." The
Springfield Missouri Patriot simply declared, "[W]e are sorry to say
that the graphic account of the terrible fight . . . is not reliable."

THE AMAZING BLACK NELL

Western papers were even more dismissive of Nichols's descriptions of Hickok's fabulous horse Black Nell. According to the article,
Hickok had trained his beautiful black mare to drop to the ground
on his command. The trick was useful during the war because it
allowed him to hide in tall grass when he came upon Confederate
enemies. "Nell laid close as a rabbit, and didn't even whisk her tail
to keep the flies off; until the rebs [rebel soldiers] moved off," Nichols's Hickok explained. Nell also seemingly understood the English
language. At one point in the profile, Wild Bill said, "That mare will
do any thing for me," and then turned to his horse and asked, "Won't
you, Nelly?" Black Nell "winked affirmatively" in response.

In another anecdote, Hickok made a bet that Nell could walk up
the steps of a saloon and climb on a billiard table and lie down. Of
course, the horse performed the trick with grace. When she came
down from the table, "Bill sprang upon her back, dashed through
the high wide doorway, and at a single bound cleared the flight of
steps and landed in the middle of the street."

The *Springfield Weekly Patriot* scoffed at the feats of this fictional Nell. Hickok's actual horse was not a mare, but a stallion. The
ragged animal was also blind in one eye. The newspaper speculated
about what might have happened if the real Nell tried to make that
jump:

> [H]e would have got a severe fall in the doorway of the
> barroom, *sure,* to make no mention of clearing at "one
> bound" a porch twelve feet wide, and five feet high, a
> pavement twelve feet, and half the width of the roadway,

(twenty-five feet by actual measurement) making a total of forty-nine feet, without computing any margin inside the room from which she (or he) "bounded."

A NEW LIFE FOR WILD BILL

Nichols's account of Hickok's Civil War adventures was also ridiculed by the *Patriot*. One tale held that Hickok with "his mate" made a daring escape on horseback from Confederate soldiers when they were behind enemy lines. Racing from their pursuers, the two riders had to jump a great ditch if they were to get away. Wild Bill "did not get a scratch," but his friend was shot and killed. The *Patriot*'s editor explained that Hickok's wartime friend, Tom Martin, the same one Nichols had claimed died at the Confederates' hands, was in fact very much alive and sitting in the editor's office. The editor explained that Martin "swore . . . that Nichols' pathetic description of his untimely murder in 1863, in that article was not true."

Most of the critics of Nichols's article assumed the author was responsible for its inaccuracies. The journalist's notes are lost, so it is actually unclear whether the fabrications were his fault or the fault of an editor's overactive imagination. Possibly, Hickok was the source of at least some of the exaggerations. He was long known by friends and family as a gifted storyteller.

There is some evidence, however, that Hickok himself was not too pleased with what Nichols had written about him. *The Army and Navy Journal* published an interview with him on April 27, 1867. In it, Hickok took exception specifically to two of Nichols's tales—the "horse story" and the description of the McCanles incident. Hickok's nephew James, the son of his brother Horace, also later recounted to Hickok biographer Joseph G. Rosa that Horace would "tell us as children how Uncle Jim would get mad when anyone mentioned the Nichols story."

Regardless of how Hickok felt about the article, it quickly had an impact on his life. Instead of a familiar western character, he was now a legend. Even his mere presence in a town became an event worthy of a mention in the local newspaper. More and more articles about Hickok appeared. Many repeated Nichols's tall tales, while others invented new ones. Like it or not, Hickok was now a public figure who, as the *Topeka Weekly Leader* wrote, had "had greatness thrust upon him."

A MAN
OF THE WEST

Despite his new celebrity, Hickok continued to work at the fairly unglamorous job of wagon master immediately after the publication of the *Harper*'s profile. In April 1867, however, he was asked to serve as a scout for a major campaign against the Cheyenne Indians. Since the end of the Civil War, the U.S. military had turned its attention to subduing the American Indians of the Great Plains. For decades, Plains Indians had lived as buffalo hunters, wandering large swatches of land in search of wild herds of these great beasts. They frequently came into conflict with non-Indians seeking to settle on lands that the American Indians considered their own. The military campaigns that made up the Plains Indian Wars of the late nineteenth century were not only an attempt to protect non-Indian settlers. They were also intended to confine conquered American Indian tribes in defined areas called reservations so that their former homelands could be opened to white homesteaders.

The campaign that Hickok joined was headed by Civil War hero General Winfield Scott Hancock. In reaction to rumors of possible American Indian attacks on Kansas settlements, the army organized the Hancock campaign to force Cheyenne leaders to negotiate with the U.S. government. With his second in command, Lieutenant Colonel George Armstrong Custer, Hancock and about 1,500 men marched through Cheyenne territory in April and May, but they encountered few American Indians. The

Hickok served as a scout for Civil War hero General Winfield Scott Hancock (*above*), a major leader of the Western frontier during the Plains Indian Wars. Under Hancock, Custer and Hickok went to war against the Cheyenne and other Plains tribes.

Cheyenne actively avoided the soldiers—a reasonable response to the 1864 Sand Creek Massacre, in which troops had slaughtered more than 100 Cheyenne and Arapaho Indians in Colorado Territory. In the end, the Hancock campaign was a disaster that exacerbated rather than calmed the growing tensions on the Plains.

TWO VIEWS OF HICKOK

Just before the Hancock campaign, Hickok was approached by another reporter eager for an interview. Henry M. Stanley was covering the Plains Indian Wars for the St. Louis newspaper *The Weekly Missouri Democrat*. Already familiar with Wild Bill from Nichols's piece, he was determined to learn more about the man he would call "one of the finest examples of that peculiar class now extant, known as Frontiersmen, ranger, hunter and Indian scout." Stanley, who would later become famous for finding the legendary Dr. David Livingston in Africa, sat down with Hickok at Fort Zarah in Kansas on April 4. Less than two weeks later, the *Democrat* published Stanley's impressions of Hickok, which only helped cement his growing reputation.

Stanley suggested that he wanted to set the record straight about his subject. He wrote that Nichols's story had been a "slight exaggeration." Wild Bill, Stanley explained, was "neither as coarse and illiterate as *Harper's* portrays him." But instead of recording an unbiased impression of the real Hickok, Stanley ended up recounting new tall tales about him. Possibly he heard these stories from Hickok himself, who might have sensed that Stanley was just a little too gullible.

Stanley's piece helped especially to advance one aspect of the Hickok legend—his image as a ruthless killer. According to the article, when Stanley asked him how many white men he had killed, Hickok responded, "I would be willing to take my oath on the Bible tomorrow that I have killed over a hundred, a long ways off." The article also offered a completely fabricated story about how he had killed his first victims. Hickok supposedly explained that one night, he was lying on a bed in a hotel room in Leavenworth when five men snuck in, intending to steal his gambling winnings. When one intruder, thinking Hickok was asleep, placed a knife to his chest, Hickok said he "sprang aside and buried mine [Hickok's knife] in his heart, and then used my revolver on the others right and left." Hickok then rushed to the nearby army fort and, with the help of soldiers there, captured the 15 surviving members of the criminal gang. According to Stanley's article, Hickok said, "We searched the cellar and found eleven bodies there—men who were murdered by those villains. . . .Would you have not done the same? That was the first man I killed, and I never was sorry for that yet."

Stanley seemed to accept the legends surrounding Hickok. But another journalist, assigned to the Hancock campaign, was far more skeptical. In an unpublished manuscript, Theodore Davis wrote how he urged Stanley to ignore the "deluges of romance with which the voluble plains man was flooding him." In Davis's eyes, Hickok was simply a bald-faced liar. He also condemned Hickok as a "dandy," a vain man overly concerned about his clothing and appearance:

> When we ordinary mortals were hustling for a clean pair of socks, . . . I have seen "Wild Bill" appear in an immaculate boiled shirt, with much collar and cuffs to match—a sleeveless Zouave jacket of startling scarlet, slashed with black velvet—The entire garment being over ornamented with buttons which if not silver seemed to be. . . . The long wavey hair that fell in masses from beneath a conventional sombrero was glossy from a recent anointment of some heavily perfumed mixture.

A DIME NOVEL HERO

A few weeks after Stanley's article was published, Hickok became the subject of a dime novel—a type of cheaply printed book that was very popular in the late nineteenth century. Publisher Robert M. De Witt released *Wild Bill, the Indian Slayer* in July 1867. Credited to "Paul Preston" (probably a pen name), it told an entirely fictitious tale of Wild Bill rescuing a white woman kidnapped by a band of

Sioux Indians. Its cover bore the same illustration used in Nichols's article to depict the McCanles incident. It was enough of a success for De Witt to issue a second Hickok book—*Wild Bill's First Trail*—in December. Although its story had no basis in fact, the book trumpeted that every word was true, making the tale far better than any "mere work of fiction could possibly be."

While others were writing and reading about his supposedly thrilling life, Hickok was struggling to find a job. His scouting work for Hancock ended in July 1867. In August, Hickok made his way to the newly established town of Ellsworth, Kansas. In its first election, he ran for marshal, but he was defeated. In November, Ellsworth

A History of the Dime Novel

In New York City in 1860, three men—Erastus Beadle, his younger brother Irwin P. Beadle, and Robert Adams—established a publishing company called Beadle & Adams. They envisioned a new form of popular entertainment, the dime novel. Dime novels, which sold for five or ten cents, were cheap books with flimsy paper covers. Inside were short novels intended to appeal to as large a segment of the public as possible. The publishers at Beadle & Adams thought that, even at their low sales price, dime novels could make money if enough copies sold.

Known by their distinctive orange covers, Beadle's Dime Novels were a phenomenal success. In just its first five years in business, Beadle & Adams sold almost 5 million books. The company went on to publish thousands of titles in more than 30 different series. Impressed by Beadle & Adams's sales numbers, other publishing companies, most notably Street & Smith, rushed to produce their own dime novel series.

Designed to appeal to a mass audience, the stories told in dime novels were fast-paced and action-packed. Many also offered a dose a humor and a gentle moral lesson. Successful writers of dime novels not only had to master this formula, but they also had to churn out manuscripts fast to meet the readers' unrelenting demands for new material. Better dime

County held another election for sheriff. Hickok ran and lost again. A piece published in *The Weekly Missouri Democrat*, however, said he came close to winning and predicted that Hickok the candidate would "bloom and blossom again."

By the end of 1867, Hickok found employment as a deputy U.S. marshal, a job he held on and off for the next three years. He also worked as a scout and possibly a saloon owner during this period. It is also likely that he tried to augment his earnings by gambling, although at the poker table he more often lost than won.

In March 1868, Hickok was in Hays City, Kansas. As a deputy marshal, he transported soldiers charged with desertion from Fort

novelists could hack out a book in just a few days. The incredibly prolific Prentiss Ingraham topped them all by supposedly writing an entire dime novel in just one day and one night.

Dime novels were written in a variety of genres. Mysteries, fantasy tales, and war stories were all popular. But particularly in the late nineteenth century, tales of heroic men and women on the western frontier held a special appeal.

Wild Bill Hickok was first immortalized by a dime novelist in 1869 in *Buffalo Bill, the King of the Border Men* (1869). The story was written by Ned Buntline (the pen name of E.Z.C. Judson), the most famous writer of dime novels. In Buntline's tale, Hickok was only a secondary character, who, to the real Hickok's chagrin, was stabbed to death by a woman. Other dime novelists, however, put Hickok front and center. His portrayal in these books furthered his fame and fleshed out the myths about his dramatic adventures in the West.

The popularity of dime novels gradually faded because of competition from pulp magazines and movies. Their influence, however, can still be seen in book series and television shows that rely on similar adventure formulas. Dime novels also transform ordinary people into memorable characters, most notably Buffalo Bill Cody and Wild Bill Hickok, who still hold an important place in American popular culture.

Hays to Hays City, where they were to stand trial. He was assisted by a well-respected scout and old friend, William F. "Buffalo Bill" Cody. Years later, in a book titled *My Life on the Frontier* (1935),

Buffalo Bill Cody was a natural showman and his exploits earned him a reputation as a national folk hero. Like Hickok, he became the subject of many dime novels based more on fiction than fact.

Miguel Otero wrote about his encounters with the two men in Hays City when he was a boy. Otero maintained that Wild Bill was "always kind and considerate toward others" and a "real joy to meet." By contrast, he thought Buffalo Bill was "rather selfish and wanted all the pomp and grandeur for himself."

During the following winter, Hickok was again employed by the U.S. Army as a scout for a new campaign in the Plains Indian Wars. In this capacity, he ran into one of his biggest detractors, Major Eugene A. Carr. Carr took an instant dislike to Hickok. He claimed Hickok had lost military dispatches he was supposed to deliver, gambled with officers, and insulted Mexican scouts working for the army by referring to them as "mongrels." In Carr's eyes, Hickok was a drunk, a liar, and a coward. Perhaps with reason, he was convinced that Hickok was a bad influence on Cody, who was then scouting for Carr. In his autobiography, Cody did later recall how, while working as scouts, he and Hickok convinced Mexican traders hauling beer to come to their camp. "The result," Cody wrote, "was one of the biggest beer jollifications it has ever been my misfortune to attend."

THE SHERIFF OF ELLIS COUNTY

In February 1869, Hickok's latest stint with the military came to an end. He would never again work as an army scout. Some accounts hold that he had been wounded in his leg by a lance during a fight with a Cheyenne Indian. In any case, he did have a leg wound when he arrived at the Hickok family home in Troy Grove, Illinois, that spring. He traveled there after his sister Lydia sent word that his mother was ill. During his visit, Lydia tended to his wound, which had become infected.

As soon as he recovered, Hickok headed back to the West. He returned to Hays City, Kansas, where he had spent time on and off for several years. At the time, Hays City was a meeting place for teamsters, buffalo hunters, and animal skinners. Many were rough men. Fistfights and even gunplay became common in the growing town. The local population demanded some protection from these outsiders. They persuaded the state government to make Hays City the seat of the newly formed Ellis County so that they could elect a county sheriff. Within months, however, the first sheriff, Thomas Gannon, disappeared—possibly because he was murdered. A succession of men took over as sheriff, but none lasted long in the job. By July 1869, the residents of Ellis County had no sheriff at all. In desperation, the county commissioners asked the government to appoint one to serve until the regular November election, but their pleas went unanswered. They then decided to take action and held their own special election. In August 1869, Wild Bill Hickok was chosen to serve as acting sheriff of Ellis County for three months.

The citizens of Hays City were happy to have Hickok as their lawman. In their eyes, his overblown reputation made him an attractive sheriff. Given all the stories of his killing ways, they figured that Hickok's presence would make outlaws think twice about coming to Hays City.

TWO FATAL ENCOUNTERS

In the end, however, some voters came to regret Hickok's election. Only a few days after he took office, Hickok was involved in a fatal shooting. Although details of the incident are murky, a report in the Kansas City paper *Daily Journal of Commerce* contended that Hickok had killed Bill Mulrey (also identified as Bill Melvin, Bill Murphy, and Bill Mulvey) "while attempting to preserve peace among a party of intoxicated roughs." Mulrey was supposedly threatening to shoot up the town when Hickok pulled out a gun and shot him in the neck and chest.

In late September, Hickok was in the middle of another violent encounter. One night, he was called to break up a near riot in John Bitter's Beer Saloon. When he got there, a man named Samuel Strawhun (also called Samuel Straughn, Samuel Strawhim, and Samuel Stranhan) and his companions were, according to the *Junction City Weekly Union*, "on a spree, and [trying] to clean out a beer saloon." About 15 men were yelling, throwing beer, and ordering so many drinks and taking them outside that there were no more glasses left in the saloon. Hickok started bringing the glasses inside when

Strawhun threatened to "shoot anyone that should try to interfere with his fun." In the bar, Strawhun held out a glass in a "threatening manner." Hickok responded by shooting him dead.

Strawhun's friends scattered, and the riot was over. The coroner investigated the shooting, and a jury found that Hickok had killed Strawhun in self-defense, even though the dead man had never drawn his gun. Although it is not entirely clear that Hickok's actions were justified, many Hays City citizens agreed with the *Leavenworth Daily Commercial*, which claimed, "Too much credit cannot be given to Wild Bill for his endeavour to rid this town of such dangerous characters as this Stranhan was."

Nevertheless, when Hickok ran for a full term as sheriff in November, he lost the election, polling 89 votes to the 114 cast for the rival candidate, Peter Lanihan. Hickok biographer Joseph G. Rosa suggests that the results are not surprising: Hickok ran as an Independent but most of the voters were Democrats, who were expected to support Lanihan, the Democratic candidate. But it is also likely that a number of voters, after witnessing a few bloody months of Hickok's brand of sheriffing, concluded that he was just a little too trigger-happy for the job.

ABILENE

After losing the election, Wild Bill Hickok left Hays City and wandered through Kansas and Missouri for several months. He spent some time in the towns of Junction City, Jefferson City, and Kansas City. He also visited Topeka, where he was arrested and fined five dollars for his part in a fistfight.

But Hays City had not seen the last of Wild Bill. By the summer, he was back and almost immediately found himself in trouble. On the evening of July 17, 1870, he was sitting in a saloon talking with the bartender when two men approached him from behind. They were Jerry Lonergan and John Kile, both privates serving in the 7th Cavalry who had sneaked out of the nearby Fort Hays for a night of carousing. According to an eyewitness, Sergeant John Ryan, Lonergan, and Kile "had some words" with Hickok just before Lonergan suddenly grabbed him and pulled him to the floor. Kile whipped out a gun, put it against Hickok's ear, and pulled the trigger. Wild Bill certainly would have been killed if Kile's gun had not, by sheer chance, misfired. Hickok managed to loosen Lonergan's grip on him just enough to pull out his own gun and start firing. He hit Lonergan in the knee, then turned and shot Kile in the arm and torso. Afraid that the soldiers' friends would come after him, Hickok ran to the back of the saloon and jumped out a window. He raced to his hotel room, gathered his things, and hightailed out of town. Kile died at Fort

Hays the following day. Lonergan's knee healed, but he was soon killed in another brawl.

The military found that Kile had been shot "in a drunken row and not in the line of duty" and took no action against Hickok. At least some citizens of Hays City, however, took a dim view of the shooting. The *Junction City Weekly Union* suggested that Hickok was right to run away because a lynch mob was hunting for him:

> The greatest excitement prevails in the town owing to the outrage. After the shooting was over Wild Bill made for the prairie and has not been heard of since. The citizens were out *en masse* looking for Bill, so that he might be summarily dealt with. The parties were all under the influence of liquor at the time.

A few months later, Hickok resurfaced in Topeka. A newspaper there reported, "Wild Bill, he of the protracted hair, and the aquiline nose, the shiny rainment and the bloody reputation, is in town."

BIRTH OF A COW TOWN

By the following spring, Hickok had found a new job. He was asked to serve as the marshal of Abilene, Kansas. Until just a few years before, Abilene had been a quiet little town. But in June 1867, Joseph G. McCoy, a cattle buyer from Illinois, bought 250 acres of land there and constructed enormous animal pens on it. McCoy was determined to transform Abilene into the first major "cow town" in the American West.

After the end of the Civil War, cattlemen had started herding up the thousands of longhorns that roamed wild in Texas and driving them north. They took several routes, but the most famous was the Chisholm Trail, which ended in Wichita, Kansas. McCoy got the idea of extending the Chisholm Trail from Wichita to Abilene and transforming the town into a shipping point. Soon, he convinced the Union Pacific Railroad to place a hundred-car switch at Abilene. In September 1867, the first trainload of cattle shipped from the

Abilene, Kansas, started as a stagecoach stop but quickly grew to be one of the biggest and wildest cow towns in the West. With the arrival of cattle traders and rowdy cowboys, entrepreneurs rushed to provide services for those willing to spend money in the town. Barbershops, saloons, restaurants, and gambling parlors enjoyed a huge jump in business.

new boomtown. The animals were transported to Chicago, Illinois, where they were slaughtered. The meat was then sent to markets in the Midwest and East. The cattle trade was very lucrative because eastern Americans seemed to have an insatiable appetite for beef.

The people of Abilene were uneasy about McCoy's venture. Many were farmers. They did not like the presence of Texas cattle in the town, because the animals carried a disease that threatened their own livestock. But even worse, the cattle were accompanied by cowboys. When these young and rowdy men came to Abilene, they were unwashed, unkempt, and exhausted after months of living on the trail. Once they delivered their herds to the pens, they flocked to the three-story Drover's Cottage hotel and prepared to spend the money they had just collected for their work. Barbers, clothing stores, and restaurants all enjoyed a jump in business when the cowboys came to town. But so did saloons, gambling parlors, and houses of prostitution. Fueled by alcohol, the cowboys were quick to get into fights or shoot off their guns just for fun.

LOOKING FOR A LAWMAN

Understandably, the permanent residents of Abilene wanted some protection from the violence and noise that visiting cowboys unleashed on the town. These citizens petitioned a judge in Dickinson County to incorporate Abilene as a city. With his approval, they were given the power to elect a mayor and a city council and to maintain a police force headed by a marshal.

Appointed in June 1870, the first marshal of Abilene was Thomas J. Smith. Respected by citizens and cowboys alike, Smith walked the streets with two pistols in his holster. But when force was needed to settle a dispute, he always used his fists rather than his guns. After serving as marshal for five months, Smith went to the house of a homesteader accused of murder. While trying to arrest the man, he took a bullet to the chest and died.

Smith was replaced with a series of unsuccessful appointees. As the cattle season of 1871 neared, Abilene's residents became nervous. They wanted a solid lawman in place when the cowboys started arriving. McCoy, who was serving as mayor, decided to offer the job to Hickok. In his book *Historical Sketches of the Cattle Trade* (1874), McCoy explained his choice: "No quiet-turned man could or would care to take the office of marshal, which jeopardized his life; hence the necessity of employing a desperado—one who feared nothing and would as soon shoot an offending subject as look at him."

McCoy's remembrance might have been colored by the Hickok legend. (He also made the outrageous claim that Hickok had killed 43 men before coming to Abilene.) But the townspeople agreed that Hickok was right for the job.

POLICING ABILENE'S STREETS

Hickok became marshal on April 15, 1871. True to form, within only a few weeks, he was involved in a controversy. When a meeting of the Abilene city council became heated, one councilman walked out. Other members called for Hickok to bring back the fleeing councilman. Soon, Hickok returned, carrying the councilman on his shoulder.

Hickok's more routine duties included making sure no one violated a ban on firearms within the city limits. Soon after the yearly arrival of the cowboys, he put up notices that he would strictly enforce the gun law. He also made sure that all gambling and prostitution was confined to one area of town to keep it away from the eyes of children. Hickok himself, however, was a regular at Abilene's saloons and gambling establishments, which led some residents to question his own sense of morality. Although he did not name Hickok, one local newspaper wrote, "It affords us no pleasure to write a word of censure against a sworn officer of the law—but when officers themselves violate, and permit its violation, it becomes the duty of the press to stand up for law and the rights of the people."

Like his predecessor, Thomas J. Smith, Hickok was not shy about using force to enforce the law. In early August, he attacked one Texas cowboy by hitting him on the head with a revolver. According to the *Kansas City Journal*, Hickok also "stamped him in the face with his boot heel, inflicting a severe wound."

SHOOTOUT AT THE ALAMO SALOON

Unlike Smith, however, Hickok was quick to draw his gun in the line of duty. On the night of October 5, a group of Texans wandered the streets, celebrating the end of the cattle season. They were stopping passersby and demanding they buy drinks for the mob. The Texans even stopped Hickok, who paid for their beers but left them with a warning to stay away from guns.

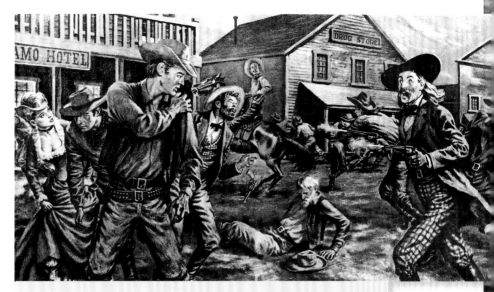

As marshal of Abilene, Hickok was responsible for making sure the streets were safe. He faced many dangers and did not hesitate to use force on unruly citizens. One such incident resulted in a shootout and the death of gambler Phil Coe (*depicted above*).

Later, Hickok heard a shot ring out. He rushed into the street and toward the direction of the sound. Outside the Alamo Saloon, he found a group of men gathered around a noted Texas gambler named Phil Coe. Coe had just taken a potshot at a stray dog.

Coe then aimed a gun at Hickok and fired twice. One bullet went through Hickok's coat; the other, between his legs. Hickok managed to pull out his two pistols and shot back. Both bullets hit Coe in the stomach. A man rushed into the fray with his gun drawn, and Hickok shot him, too. It was too dark for Hickok to see that the man was his friend Mike Williams, who was just trying to come to Hickok's aid. Hickok picked up Williams's body, carried it into the Alamo, and laid it out on the billiards table. He then went outside and told the crowd to disperse. Coe's companions took him to a nearby house, where he suffered in agony for three days before he also died.

According to the *Junction City Weekly Union*, the people of Abilene supported Hickok's actions: "[T]he verdict of the citizens seemed to be unanimously in support of the Marshal, who bravely did his duty." In Texas, though, Hickok was widely condemned. One Texas paper called him "the terror of the West" and maintained that the "gallows and penitentiary are the places to tame such blood thirsty wretches as 'Wild Bill.'" It is possible that some Texans offered a reward to anyone who would murder Hickok. A few weeks after

Wild Bill Hickok and Phil Coe

Because of the high demand for building materials, Theophilus Little established a lumberyard in the fast-growing cattle town of Abilene, Kansas, in March 1871. He later recorded his memories of the place in an essay titled "Early Days of Abilene and Dickinson County." In it, Little provided his impressions of Wild Bill Hickok's deadly clash with Texas gambler Phil Coe.

In the spring of 1871 Wild Bill was appointed City Marshall of Abilene. He was made Marshall because of his known ability to handle "bad men." Bad men feared him, good citizens looked to him for protection.

"Phil" Coe was from Texas and run a low down gambling den, on Texas Street. He was a red mouthed, bawling "thug"—"plug" Ugly—a very dangerous beast. For some reason Wild Bill had incurred his violent hatred and Coe planned to kill him or rather to have him killed, being too cowardly to do it himself. One afternoon Coe got about 200 of the cowboys crazy drunk, his plan being to have them commit some overt act. The Marshall would arrest some of them—being so drunk they were to resist, start the shooting and kill the Marshall. Some friend informed the Marshall of the plot.

I remember the evening so well. About dusk I left my office to go to the Gulf House on my way home. I saw this band of crazy men. They went up and down the street with a wild swish and rush and

Coe's death, Hickok, while in Topeka, did in fact get wind of a plan to kill him. With his pistols drawn, Hickok met the would-be assassins as they arrived in the city by train. Holding them at gunpoint, he told them to stay exactly where they were. The train left Topeka with the killers still aboard.

With the end of the cattle season, Abilene again grew quiet. While McCoy was out of town, the city council told Hickok his services were no longer needed. Hickok drew a large salary, and some

roar, totally oblivious to anything in their path. . . . The howling mob gathered around but Wild Bill had singled out Phil Coe, who had his gun out, but the Marshall had his two deadly guns leveled on Coe and pulled a trigger of each gun and just at that instant a policeman [Mike Williams] rushed around the corner of the building right between the guns and Coe and he received both bullets and fell dead. The Marshall instantly pulled two triggers again and two lead balls entered Coe's abdomen. Whirling on the mob his two 44 six shooters drawn on them, he calmly said, "If any of you want the balance of these pills, come and get them." Not a word was uttered, they were sobered and paralyzed. . . . Coe did not die that night, and this son of a Presbyterian Elder, Wild Bill, got a preacher out of bed and had him go to the dying gambler, Phil Coe, and pray with and for him. He died the next day.

The police man whom the Marshall killed was the son of a widow of Kansas City, Missouri. He sent money to the mother to come to Abilene, procured a fine burial casket, had a large funeral and shipped the body to Kansas City for burial, paying all expenses.

I felt a great sense of relief when I learned that Phil Coe was dead. He owned me $40 for a bill of lumber. I had asked him to pay and he was very abusive and I was always afraid that he would burn me out. He owes the bill yet, and I don't want to go where he is to get it.

councilmen were upset by his drinking and gambling. But even more important, they no longer needed a lawman to protect them from the yearly surge of cowboys. The councilmen were already making plans to ban the cattle trade from Abilene. The disruption was too great, and they decided that the real future of the town lay in farming. After just eight months as marshal of Abilene, Hickok once again found himself without a job.

ON STAGE

After leaving Abilene, Wild Bill Hickok spent most of his time in Kansas City, Missouri. His main occupation was gambling. Every day, just after noon, the people of the town could expect to see Hickok emerge from his hotel and walk to the Marble Hall, his favorite gambling parlor, for a game of poker.

THE GREAT BUFFALO HUNT

During the summer of 1872, Hickok's regular routine was interrupted by a visit from Colonel Sidney Barnett. Barnett's father owned a museum near Niagara Falls, the great waterfalls on the Niagara River that separate New York State from Ontario in Canada. Niagara Falls was already a popular tourist destination, but Barnett wanted to attract American tourists to the Canadian side of the falls by putting on a spectacular show there.

Barnett's production was an early version of what would become known as a Wild West show. Appealing especially to readers of dime novels, these outdoor shows became popular in the late nineteenth century. The shows capitalized on eastern Americans' interest in tall tales about the western frontier and often featured the real people whom the novels glorified as heroes.

Barnett had first hired John "Texas Jack" Omohundro, an old friend of Hickok's, but Omohundro backed out when Barnett refused to feature a few of his Pawnee Indian friends in the show because the United States would not let them cross the border into Canada. Barnett then sought out Hickok in Kansas City. Wild Bill agreed to act as the master of ceremonies for Barnett's extravaganza.

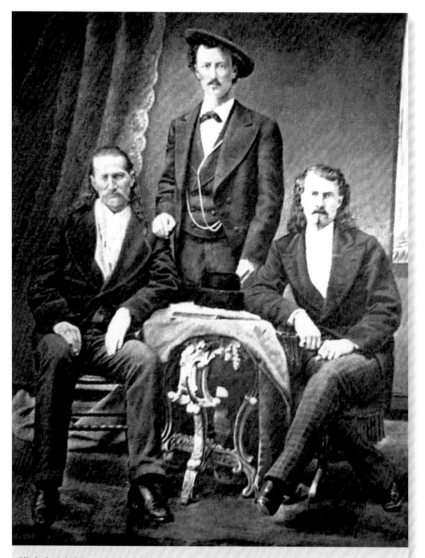

Hickok (*right*) toured with his friends Buffalo Bill Cody (*left*) and Texas Jack Omohundro (*center*) in one of the original Wild West plays, *Scouts of the Plains*. After Hickok and Texas Jack left the show, Buffalo Bill would go on to form his famous Buffalo Bill's Wild West, a circuslike show that toured annually.

Never the most talented gambler, Hickok was likely motivated to take the job more by a lack of cash than by a genuine attraction to show business.

Two performances of Barnett's show were staged on August 28 and 30. It was called the "Great Buffalo Hunt," although the show featured only three of these Great Plains animals. More impressive than Barnett's meager buffalo herd were the cowboy entertainers, who displayed their lassoing skills, and American Indian performers, who danced and played traditional ball games. Despite plenty of publicity, the public response to the "Great Buffalo Hunt" was mixed. Hickok was happy to return to Kansas City after his eastern adventure was over.

On September 27, Hickok was involved in another incident that attracted the attention of local papers. While he was attending a fair known as the Kansas City Exposition, a group of Texans asked a band to play the song "Dixie." It was a favorite tune of the Confederates during the Civil War. Because of its association with the Confederacy, several audience members asked the musicians to stop, but the Texans pulled out their guns to force the band to keep playing. Hickok, a devoted Union man, then stepped forward and demanded that the bandmaster stop the music. According to the *Topeka Daily Commonwealth*, about 50 men aimed their pistols at Hickok, "but he came away unscathed."

Wild Bill again made news in March 1873. That month, several newspapers reported a rumor that he had been assassinated at Fort Dodge in Iowa. Hickok sent a wry note to the *Springfield Advertiser*. It read, "I hereby acknowledge that I am dead." The *Springfield Times* reprinted his response and could not resist adding, "We suppose he means dead drunk." When the news of his supposed murder spread, Hickok felt compelled to stop the rumor by writing to the editors of two papers in St. Louis to confirm he was still very much alive.

AN OFFER FROM BUFFALO BILL

A few months later, Hickok's old friend Buffalo Bill Cody convinced him to take another crack at show business. Hoping to score some quick money, Wild Bill again traveled east to perform with Cody and Omohundro in "Cody's Combination." Cody was a natural performer, but Hickok seemed to hate appearing before an audience. As Cody later wrote in his autobiography, Wild Bill "had a fine stage appearance and was a handsome fellow, and possessed a good strong voice, yet when he went upon the stage before an audience, it was almost impossible for him to utter a word. He insisted that we were making a set of fools of ourselves, and that we were the laughing-stock of the people." Hickok all too often took his frustration and embarrassment out on the cast and crew. He enjoyed shooting blanks at the performers playing American Indians, painfully burning their legs. He also once became so angry at a crewmember who turned a spotlight on his face that he shattered the light with a bullet.

For all of his crankiness, Hickok remained a favorite of audiences. According to Cody, "If Wild Bill was not a star on the stage, he was a sensation off it. Crowds followed him about everywhere. I didn't wonder at it, for aside from his picturesque Western garb, he was one of the handsomest men I ever knew."

By March 1874, Hickok had had enough. During an engagement in Rochester, New York, he abruptly left the show. Although it is not entirely clear whether he quit or was fired, one story holds that he parted from Cody and Omohundro as friends. They each supposedly gave him $500 and a pistol as gestures of thanks for his help with the show. Hickok probably joined another western show in New York City but soon quit it as well. When the show hired another actor to play him, legend has it that he was so mad, he disrupted a performance by throwing his replacement off the stage.

Hickok told a reporter that he quit Cody's show because he had received a telegram from General Philip Sheridan. The general wanted him to return to scouting for the army at Fort Laramie in Wyoming Territory. In all likelihood, Hickok made the story up to save face. Captain Jack Crawford, a pal of Hickok's, offered decades later to the *New York Journalist* another, more romantic explanation for Hickok's fizzled show business career: "He hated hypocrisy and fraud and that was why he said he would rather go back to the

West and get killed than accept $500 per week and play in a dime novel melodrama which was a libel on the West and destined only to ruin credulous boys." Most likely, though, the truth was simpler.

Scouts of the Plains, starring Buffalo Bill Cody, Texas Jack, Wild Bill Hickok, and Italian actress Giuseppina Morlacchi as an innocent Indian heroine, toured the country's eastern cities. The newspaper reviews were dismal, Hickok often forgot his lines or made up his own, and frequently the cast was involved in barroom brawls in various town saloons after the shows.

Buffalo Bill's Wild West

In 1873, Wild Bill Hickok got a taste of show business and found it was not to his liking. His friend William F. "Buffalo Bill" Cody, on the other hand, embraced the stage. Although he had been a famed army scout, Buffalo Bill's greatest achievement was his development of a new form of entertainment—the Wild West show.

Buffalo Bill became an entertainer only after he met author E.Z.C. Judson at Fort McPherson in Nebraska in 1869. Judson, who went by the pen name Ned Buntline, was already a prolific writer of dime novels. He saw in Cody the makings of a perfect western character. In a series of stories and novels, Buntline created a fictional Buffalo Bill, a heroic western adventurer only very loosely based on Cody himself.

In 1872, Cody made a trip to New York City, where he again met Buntline. The author suggested he attend a play there based on Buntline's novel *Buffalo Bill, the King of the Border Men* (1869). When the cast discovered that the real Buffalo Bill was in the audience, he was asked to step on stage and take a bow. From that modest beginning, Cody built a show business career. For the next 10 years, he spent much of his time playing himself in theatrical productions.

In 1883, Cody and a partner launched their own show. The impressive production, eventually called Buffalo Bill's Wild West, featured a variety of

Hickok was not a shy man. He enjoyed wearing fancy clothing and telling fantastic stories to groups of enthralled listeners. But unlike his friend Cody, he was not enough of an exhibitionist to enjoy presenting a fictional version of himself, night after night, to an adoring crowd.

BACK IN THE WEST

After the debacle with "Cody's Combination," Hickok returned to the West. His movements in late 1874 are not well documented.

acts and performances, all designed to give audiences a sense of life in the "real" American West. The show included displays of sharpshooting, cattle roping, trick riding, and horse racing. It also showcased dramatic recreations of the type of scenes from dime novels familiar to the crowds. For instance, a consistent crowd-pleaser was a choreographed attack on a Deadwood stagecoach. To bolster his claim to give audiences "actual scenes, genuine characters," Cody often hired western acquaintances to play versions of themselves on stage. One of his most famous performers was the Lakota Sioux leader Sitting Bull. During the show's 1885 season, Sitting Bull rode a gray circus horse through the arena during each performance as the audience cheered.

Cody's extravaganza was not the first show to focus on western performers and characters, but it was the most successful Wild West show. For decades, it toured the United States and Europe. During that time, Buffalo Bill's Wild West spawned dozens of imitators, each of which presented its own fictional version of the West to audiences who would never know the real thing.

A year after Cody's death in 1917, his Wild West shows came to an end. By that time, the popularity of these entertainments was on the wane. They were being replaced by rodeos, contests in which participants competed in events such as calf roping and bronco riding. Still today, rodeos draw large crowds throughout the American West.

During this time, he probably served as a scout for a group of wealthy European tourists.

Most likely, Hickok spent much of his time in Cheyenne, a town in Wyoming Territory. On June 17, 1875, he was arrested there for vagrancy. The leaders in the city had tagged Hickok as an undesirable, probably because he was spending much of his time gambling and drinking. Rather than the fighting man depicted in novels and articles about him, Hickok, according to one paper, had become "a very tame and worthless loafer and bummer." But, according to the *Cheyenne Daily Leader*, his behavior was not so tame during his vagrancy arrest: "Bill cordially invited the officer to go to a much warmer clime than this, and expressed the intention of staying here as long as he pleased."

In 1875, however, Hickok likely left Cheyenne to visit Kansas City. Many accounts hold that Hickok's eyesight was failing. It is speculated that he went to Kansas City to consult with an eye doctor there.

Hickok was back in Cheyenne in 1876. Also there was a woman named Agnes Lake Thatcher, who was a noted performer. With her late husband, she had traveled across the United States and Europe with a circus act. Thatcher had met Hickok in Abilene on one of her tours five years before. They had since occasionally exchanged letters. When Hickok found out she was in Cheyenne to see her friend Minnie Moyer, he went to pay her a visit.

On March 5, 1876, Hickok and Thatcher were married in the Moyer home by Reverend W.R. Warren. Warren curiously wrote in the church register, "I don't think the[y] meant it." But years later, Agnes Hickok claimed theirs had been a true romance. "It is impossible for a human being to Love any better than what I did him," she said.

The couple honeymooned first in St. Louis, Missouri, and then in Cincinnati, Ohio, where the Hickoks visited relatives of Agnes. After two weeks, Hickok again left for the West. One journalist held that Hickok did not like being married, although he seemed content to spend his wife's money. One of his nephews, Howard L. Hickok, later claimed that Wild Bill disliked living off Agnes's savings. He said Hickok wanted to find a way to financially support his bride. At the time, for anyone like Hickok who wanted to make a fortune and make it fast, there was one obvious place to go—the Black Hills of what is now South Dakota. In 1874, an army expedition led by Lieutenant Colonel George Armstrong Custer had journeyed to the Black Hills and discovered gold in the remote region.

TO THE BLACK HILLS

Hickok's original idea for making money off the Black Hills gold rush was to act as a guide for would-be prospectors. He printed a circular touting the "Black Hills and Bighorn Expedition." Originating in St. Louis, the expedition was to travel to Cheyenne and from there into gold country. In addition to the cost of food and supplies, each traveler would pay Hickok a fee of $25 to $33. Originally, the expedition was supposed to leave St. Louis in May, but the date was soon pushed back to June. However, when June arrived, Hickok was hanging around Cheyenne, hundreds of miles from St. Louis. His moneymaking scheme seemed to have fallen apart. Perhaps he did not attract enough customers; a rival company might have siphoned off enough to make his venture unprofitable. Or, perhaps his health was failing, making him unfit for the grueling work of a guide.

For whatever reason he put off his expedition, Hickok reunited with an old friend, Charlie Utter, while in Cheyenne. Utter was eager to start a freighting service into the Black Hills. Together with Utter's brother Steve, the two men decided late in June to head off to the gold rush town of Deadwood. (It had earned its eerie name from the large number of blackened dead tress on the hills nearby.) They were accompanied by a man known as Pie and by Joseph Foster Anderson and his brother Charley. Joseph was better known by the colorful nickname "White Eye." One of his eyebrows had been burned off by a hot cinder, only to grow back totally white.

By early July, the travelers had reached Fort Laramie. There, soldiers cautioned them to join a larger party for their own safety. In the last week of June, the entire 7th Cavalry of the U.S. Army, headed by Hickok's old friend Lieutenant Colonel George Armstrong Custer, had been slaughtered by Lakota and Cheyenne warriors at the Battle of the Little Bighorn. The most dramatic defeat of the U.S. military during the Plains Indian Wars, the event had set all non-Indians in the western frontier lands on edge.

Also at Fort Laramie, Hickok's party met up with Martha Canary, who would become better known as Calamity Jane. At the time, she was locked up in the guardhouse after a night of drinking with some soldiers. Jane was an acquaintance of Steve Utter, so the officer asked Hickok's party to take her out of Fort Laramie. According to the memoirs of White Eye Anderson, they all gave her some men's clothing made of buckskin to replace her tattered dress. Once

A few years after meeting Wild Bill Hickok, Calamity Jane became a famous heroine of dime novels. Among those who knew her, however, she was best-known for dressing in men's clothing, chronic drunkenness, and eccentric behavior.

she "got cleaned up and sober," Anderson wrote, she "looked quite attractive." (He also admired her "wonderful command of profanity.") Anderson claimed that Jane was "a big-hearted woman and she and I became good friends." Hickok, on the other hand, "surely did not have any use for her." She apparently annoyed him by drinking up too much of the whiskey he had brought for the trip.

With Jane in tow, Hickok and his friends joined about 30 other wagons that were heading into the Black Hills. Given the volatile situation between whites and Plains Indians, the move was prudent. But no amount of care could completely protect Hickok as he headed into Deadwood, where he was destined to live the final chapter of his life.

8

DEADWOOD

By mid-July 1876, Wild Bill Hickok and his friends arrived in Deadwood. Nestled in the northern Black Hills, the town was one of the wildest in the West. Dozens of saloons, dance halls, and gambling parlors along its main street operated all day and all night to cater to its rough population of miners and gamblers. At the town's height, its Gem Theater sold $10,000 worth of tickets a night.

Despite Hickok's fame, the local paper was more excited that Calamity Jane had come to town. In a mining settlement where women were scarce, the arrival of a potential dance hall girl was certain to attract attention. In Deadwood, the arrival of one more hard-drinking, aging gambler like Hickok seemed like nothing special.

Even Hickok's reputation as a lawman received little attention in Deadwood. Law and order was not a high priority for its residents. In fact, Deadwood itself was an illegal settlement. It was within the borders of the Great Sioux Reservation, which was established by an 1868 treaty between the Lakota Sioux and the U.S. government. The reservation included a large swath of present-day South Dakota and small portions of what are now Nebraska and North Dakota. According to the terms of the treaty, the area was supposed to be for the exclusive use of the Lakota Indians. The hardened residents of Deadwood, however, were uninterested in treaty rights. They cared about little aside from the mad rush for gold.

After Lieutenant Colonel George Armstrong Custer announced the discovery of gold in the Black Hills of what is now the state of South Dakota, men began arriving in droves in the town of Deadwood. The population quickly grew and the town became known for its lawlessness. Pictured is a view of the main street in 1877.

HANGING OUT IN A MINING TOWN

With several of his traveling companions, Hickok set up camp outside of Deadwood along the Whitewood Creek. On July 17, he wrote to his wife, eager to let her know he was already hard at work in the gold fields: "I never was as well in my life but you would laughf [*sic*] to see me now. Just got in from Prospecting will go away to morrow. Will writ In the morning."

More likely, he spent most of his time hanging around camp practicing his shooting or in town frequenting one of its many drinking and gambling establishments. In his memoirs, White Eye Anderson described Hickok's morning routine at camp, which hardly seemed like that of a man serious about spending the day prospecting: "The first thing Wild Bill would do in the morning was empty his pistols in target practice at an old cottonwood tree that grew on the bank of the creek, then he would take a stiff drink of whiskey and he would be ready for breakfast."

A Massachusetts journalist named Leander Richardson also left a record of Hickok's life in Deadwood. Richardson's overblown praise for Hickok suggests he was more interested in securing Wild Bill's legend than in creating an accurate portrait of the man. (For instance, at one point in his article titled "Last Days of a Plainsman," Richardson grandly wrote, "Of course I had heard of him, the greatest scout in the West, but I was not prepared to find such a man as he proved to be.")

Richardson's romanticized remembrances, however, did at least shed some light on Hickok's friendship with Charlie Utter. Like many people who met Hickok, Richardson was impressed by his clothing: "His costume was a courisly [*sic*] blended union of the habiliments of the borderman and the drapery of the fasionable dandy." But Richardson claimed Utter was even more meticulous about his appearance. He liked to dress in beaded moccasins, fringed leggings, and a belt with a big silver buckle. Utter also took a bath each morning. Daily bathing was apparently so uncommon in Deadwood that "people used to come out and view the process with interest not wholly unmixed with wonder." Richardson suggested that Calamity Jane had much more of a romantic interest in the clean and nicely dressed Utter than she did in Hickok.

Hickok and Utter seemed to have had a combative relationship. Richardson wrote, "I never heard anybody take 'roastings' with as little concern as that with which Bill used to take the fierce tongue lashings of his dudesque little partner." Utter was also willing to strike back when Hickok did something that annoyed him. Once, Hickok returned to camp from a saloon and decided to take a nap on Utter's carefully arranged and laundered bed clothes. When Utter saw Hickok, he became furious and dragged his drunken friend out of his tent by his feet. Utter then immediately grabbed his blankets and hung them on a tree to air out.

DEATH AT A POKER TABLE

On August 1, Hickok was in Deadwood, playing cards as usual. Another player was a 25-year-old man named Jack McCall. When McCall lost all his money, Hickok offered to pay for the young man's breakfast.

The next afternoon, Hickok was back at the poker table. At the Nuttall & Mann's No. 10 Saloon, he was playing with his friends Carl Mann, Charles Rich, and Captain Massie. Hickok sat with his back facing the front door. At about 3:00 P.M., McCall walked in and went to the bar before sidling up behind Hickok. Suddenly, McCall shouted, "Damn you, take that!" Hickok's head jerked forward, and then his body fell sideways to the floor. Wild Bill Hickok was dead, killed instantly by a single bullet to the back of his head.

McCall pointed his gun at the shocked onlookers, threatening to shoot anyone who tried to stop him as he backed out through the saloon's rear door. Outside, he tried to get on his horse. The saddle's girth (the band that held it to the animal's belly) was not pulled tight enough. The saddle slipped to the side, and McCall fell on the ground. Scrambling to his feet, he ran inside Shoudy's, a butcher shop. There, an angry crowd cornered him and took him prisoner.

On August 2, 1876, Hickok would play his last game of poker at Nuttal and Mann's Saloon No. 10. As legend has it, he broke his own rule by sitting with his back to the door, and was killed instantly from a shot in the back of the head. The cards he was holding—two black aces and eights and a jack or queen of diamonds—became known as a "dead man's hand."

He was locked up in a cabin while the people of Deadwood tried to figure out what to do next.

Some of Hickok's friends talked about hanging McCall, but cooler heads decided to give him a trial. The town of Deadwood had no real legal system, so the citizens had to improvise. They chose a man named Isaac Brown to act as sheriff. He was responsible for guarding McCall. Then they selected a judge, W.I. Kuykendall, to oversee the trial, as well as a prosecuting attorney, a defense lawyer, and a jury.

The trial began at 9:00 on the morning after Hickok's murder. Carl Mann, Charles Rich, and Harry "Sam" Young, the bartender at the saloon, all offered eyewitness testimony. McCall's defense hinged on his contention that Hickok had killed McCall's brother back in Kansas. Perhaps because of Hickok's public reputation as a killer, the jury believed McCall's story. Seeing a revenge murder as being morally justified, it found McCall not guilty. McCall undoubtedly knew that the verdict would not sit well with Hickok's friends. To escape their wrath, he quickly left Deadwood.

BURYING A LEGEND

While McCall was defending himself, Charlie Utter made funeral arrangements for his dead friend. He circulated a notice that the funeral would be held at his camp on the afternoon of August 3. According to Leander Richardson, the brief service drew "hundreds of rough miners standing around the bier with bowed heads and tear-dimmed eyes." A correspondent from the *Chicago Inter-Ocean* noted that Hickok's corpse was "a picture of perfect repose. . . . His long chestnut hair, evenly parted over his marble brow, hung in waving ringlets over the broad shoulders; his face was cleanly shaved excepting the drooping mustache, which shaded a mouth which in death almost seemed to smile, but which in life was unusually grave." The report said that a rifle was buried with Hickok, according to his "often expressed desire."

On August 5, the *Deadwood Black Hills Pioneer* provided the first published account of Hickok's death. Soon after, the story ran in papers in Hickok's old haunts of Cheyenne, Hays City, and Abilene. After the appearance of a graphic account in the *Chicago Inter-Ocean*, the news spread across the country.

Several popular stories grew up around Hickok's murder. Some accounts said that Hickok, recognizing the many enemies he had made, always insisted on a seat against the wall whenever he played

The Burial of Wild Bill

John Wallace Crawford was famed as an army scout, a journalist, and a Wild West show performer. But he was perhaps best known as the "poet scout." In his 1879 book of poems by that name, Crawford wrote verses about famous western figures, such as William F. "Buffalo Bill" Cody, Lieutenant Colonel George Armstrong Custer, and General George Crook. The volume featured three poems about Wild Bill Hickok, including the mournful "Burial of Wild Bill." Dedicated to Charlie Utter, it was written before Jack McCall's second trial and execution. In the last verse, Crawford imagines Wild Bill one day traveling from heaven to hell to wreak revenge on his murderer.

Under the sod in the prairie-land
    We have laid him down to rest,
With many a tear from the sad,
rough throng
    And the friends he loved the
    best;
And many a heart-felt sigh was
heard
    As over the earth we trod,
And many an eye was filled with
tears
    As we covered him with the sod.

Under the sod in the prairie-land
    We have laid the good and the
    true—
An honest heart and a noble scout
    Has bade us a last adieu.
No more his silvery laugh will ring,
    His spirit has gone to God;
Around his faults let Charity cling
    While you cover him with the sod.

Under the sod in the land of gold
    We have laid the fearless bill;

cards. On the fateful day in Nuttall & Mann's No. 10 Saloon, Hickok supposedly asked Charles Rich to change seats with him, but Rich refused. If only Rich had accommodated his friend, the story suggested dramatically, Hickok would still be alive.

Other reports of Hickok's death said he had predicted his life was near its end. *The Cheyenne Daily Leader*, for instance, held that just a week before the murder, Hickok said, "I feel that my days

We called him Wild, yet a little child
Could bend his iron will.
With generous heart he freely gave
To the poorly clad, unshod—
Think of it, pards—of his noble
traits—
While you cover him with the
sod.

Under the sod in Deadwood Gulch
You have laid his last remains;
No more his manly form will hail
The red man on the plains.
And, Charley, may Heaven bless
you!
You gave him a "bully good
send";
Bill was a friend to you, pard,
And you were his last, best
friend.

You buried him 'neath the old pine
tree,
In that little world of ours,
His trusty rifle by his side—
His grave all strewn with flowers;

His manly form in sweet repose,
That lovely silken hair
I tell you, pard, it was a sight,
That face so white and fair!

And while he sleeps beneath the
sod
His murderer goes free,
Released by a perjured, gaming set,
Who'd murder you and me—
Whose coward hearts dare never
meet
A brave man on the square.
Well, pard, they'll find a warmer
clime
Than they ever found out there.

Hell is full of just such men;
And if Bill is above to-day,
The Almighty will have enough to do
To keep him from going away—
That is, from making a little scout
To the murderers' home below;
And if old Peter will let him out,
He can clean out the ranch, I
know.

are numbered; my sun is sinking fast, I know I shall be killed here, something tells me I shall never leave these hills alive."

Perhaps the most enduring myth about the death of Hickok is the story of the poker game. Supposedly, when he was shot by McCall, his poker hand fell to the floor. By most accounts, it included two black aces, two black eights, and the jack or queen of diamonds. Still today, this combination of cards is known as the "dead man's hand." There is no evidence, however, that Hickok was holding this exact hand.

THE END OF JACK MCCALL

Many tales also arose to explain the most enduring mystery surrounding Hickok's murder: Why did Jack McCall do it? The least satisfying explanations are probably the most likely. Drunk and mad about losing at cards to Hickok, he might just have impulsively killed a man he barely knew. Perhaps McCall just wanted the notoriety that would surely come to the shooter who took down Wild Bill.

For many Americans, the idea that Hickok was killed on a whim by the likes of Jack McCall did not sit well. After all, McCall hardly seemed a worthy adversary of the great Wild Bill. A drifter who went by several aliases, he was called "brutish," "cross-eyed," and "snub-nosed" in the press. Resisting the idea that Hickok died at the hands of such a pathetic man acting alone, admirers of Wild Bill wanted to believe McCall was part of a larger conspiracy. Some people claimed that Deadwood was going to make Hickok marshal. By this theory, a band of criminals, afraid that Hickok would bring law and order to the raucous mining town, ordered his assassination. However, in the historical record, there is no suggestion that Hickok was asked to serve as Deadwood's marshal. John S. McClintock, who had been in Deadwood at the time of Hickok's death, later declared in his book *Pioneer Days in the Black Hills* (1939) that the idea of a conspiracy was merely cooked up by "hero worshipers for the purpose of leading readers into belief that their hero was greatly feared by the tough element in Deadwood."

McCall was able to flee from Deadwood, but in the end he was not able to escape justice. He traveled first to Cheyenne and then to Laramie City, where he was arrested by a deputy U.S. marshal. The Deadwood trial, in a makeshift court outside the jurisdiction of the United States, was deemed illegitimate. McCall was therefore taken to Yankton, Dakota Territory, to be tried in federal court. The court sent for witnesses from Deadwood, while Lorenzo Hickok arrived to watch the trial of his brother's killer.

In Yankton, McCall's defense fell apart. His claim that Hickok had killed his brother was proved false when someone who knew McCall from childhood testified that he did not even have a brother. That and the eyewitness testimony convinced the jury that McCall was guilty. In early January 1877, he was sentenced to death.

His defense attorney wanted to have the sentence commuted, or reduced. He trafficked the idea that Hickok was a bad and violent man, so clearly McCall had acted in self-defense. The prosecuting attorney expressed umbrage at this attack on Hickok's character. He defended Hickok by reminding the court of Hickok's Civil War record, specifically his "fearless and efficient service as a Union Scout." In the end, the conviction stood. On March 1, 1877, Jack McCall was hanged in Yankton. The killer of the legendary Wild Bill Hickok was now himself dead at the hands of the law.

LEGACY AND LEGEND

In September 1877, Agnes Lake Thatcher Hickok came to Deadwood to visit her husband's grave. Its head was marked with a tree stump carved with a simple epitaph: "A brave man; the victim of an assassin—J.B. (Wild Bill) Hickock, aged 48 years; murdered by Jack McCall, August 2, 1876." She was accompanied on her trip by a man named George Carson. They soon took out a marriage license, but it is unknown if they ever wed. Until her death in 1907, however, she continued to call herself Mrs. James B. Hickok.

Agnes Hickok considered moving Hickok's body to Cincinnati, but in the end she chose to leave his remains where they were. Three years after his death, however, the town of Deadwood decided to disinter Wild Bill. The town was growing fast and wanted to develop the land where Hickok was buried. Charlie Utter came to Deadwood to oversee the exhuming of the body and its reburial in the Mount Moriah Cemetery.

A POPULAR GRAVESITE

The tree stump headstone was set up at the new grave, but it did not remain in place for long. Even after his death, Hickok was a famous

Calamity Jane, photographed posing near Wild Bill Hickok's grave, was buried next to him in 1903. Late in life, she improbably alleged that she had been engaged to Hickok when he died. In 1941, a woman named Jean Hickok McCormick made national news with an even more unbelievable claim: She said she was the long lost daughter of Jane and Wild Bill. The diaries of Calamity Jane she produced were later deemed to be fakes.

man. Visitors to Deadwood always stopped by Hickok's grave. Many helped themselves to souvenirs by chipping away at pieces of wood from the headstone until it was nearly shaved away. A series of stone replacements were also destroyed by tourists who wanted to take home a bit of Wild Bill.

The popularity of the gravesite was not unnoticed by the cemetery's owners. They made the false claim that Utter had not fully paid for Hickok's plot, and they began negotiating with an agent representing a museum in New York City that wanted to buy and display Hickok's corpse. Utter had to race to Deadwood with documentation of the plot's sale to stop them.

In 1903, Will Bill Hickok got a new neighbor. At the age of 50, Calamity Jane died and was buried near him. The two in death became united in a way they had never been in life. Wild Bill and Jane had actually known each other only a few weeks, and during that time they were not close. Even calling their acquaintance a friendship was something of a stretch. Calamity Jane herself acknowledged that was the case in her 1896 autobiography, *Life and Adventures of Calamity Jane, by Herself.*

But by 1902, she had a different story. She told a reporter in Aberdeen, South Dakota, that she and Hickok were engaged when he was murdered. Soon before she died, Jane was photographed standing by his grave. Calamity Jane, seeing that Hickok's fame only seemed to be growing, probably hoped she would somehow be able to profit from exaggerating her connection to Wild Bill.

THE NOVELS OF J.W. BUEL

In the years immediately following Hickok's death, the person most responsible for fueling his legend was J.W. Buel. A former journalist, Buel possibly once met Hickok in St. Louis, where he was the editor of a local paper. Buel published his first book about Hickok in 1880. Its grandiose title was *The Life and Marvelous Adventures of Wild Bill, the Scout, Being a True and Exact History of All the Sanguinary Combats and Hair-Breadth Escapes of the Most Famous Scout and Spy America Ever Produced.* The book was so popular that the following year it spawned a sequel, *Heroes of the Plains; or, Lives and Wonderful Adventures of Wild Bill, Buffalo Bill, Kit Carson, Capt. Payne, "White Beaver," Capt. Jack, Texas Jack, California Joe, and Other Celebrated Indian Fighters, Scouts, Hunters and Guides.*

Buel claimed his portrayal of Hickok was "absolutely true in every particular, without a single shading of fiction or extravagance." To bolster his claim, he sprinkled his narrative with quotations from Hickok's own journal, which Buel said Hickok's widow had given him. (No such journal is known to have existed.) Contrary to Buel's characterization of his work as "truthful history," his novels consisted of little more than stories recycled from Nichols's untrustworthy article with a few new myths of Buel's invention.

Among Buel's most important additions to the Hickok legend was his portrayal of Wild Bill as a cool and clever trickster who used his wits to get himself out of trouble. In one story recounted by Buel, an outlaw had two revolvers trained at Hickok's head. Calmly, Hickok shouted to some imaginary assailants, "Boys, don't hit him." Afraid he was about to be struck down, the outlaw turned to see who Hickok was talking to, giving Hickok the chance to pull his gun and shoot him. In another story, Hickok was in a restaurant, where he ordered a bowl of oyster stew. When the waiter was about to serve him, one of Hickok's old enemies charged in with a gun in his hand, but Hickok shot him before the man had a chance to pull the trigger. In the chaos, the waiter dropped the stew. Completely unruffled, Hickok retook his seat and ordered another bowl as though nothing unusual had happened.

Buel also emphasized Hickok's role as a lawman. Past novels about Hickok had highlighted his skills as a scout and his role in the Civil War. Later accounts, like Buel's, were more interested in the idea of Hickok as a tamer of the West, as a man who brought civilization to a lawless region. Modern historians have shown that such writings about the "Wild West" tended to grossly exaggerate the amount of violence in western towns. Perhaps the authors felt they had to make their western villains unrealistically evil to justify their heroes' violent acts against them. Because the memories of the real carnage during the Civil War and Plains Indian Wars were still fresh in the minds of many Americans in the late nineteenth century, the cartoonish violence in books like Buel's made readers feel more comfortable than a more realistic depiction would have. And by recasting Hickok and other western heroes as civilizers, readers could feel that all those shootings were the service of a greater and necessary goal.

Like Buel, later writers about Hickok's life often combined old stories with new ones of their own. Among the many books about

Hickok published long after his death were *Wild Bill, the Pistol Prince* (1891) by Prentiss Ingraham, *The Story of the Outlaw* (1907) by Emerson Hough, *Wild Bill Hickok: The Prince of Pistoleers* (1926) by Frank J. Wilstach, *The Real Wild Bill Hickok* (1931) by Wilbert E. Eisele, and *Wild Bill Hickok* (1959) by Richard O'Connor. Some of these books billed themselves as biographies rather than novels, although their stories were still largely fictional.

WILD BILL AND CALAMITY JANE

John S. McClintock's *Pioneer Days in the Black Hills*, published in 1921, played a special role in the evolving mythology surrounding Wild Bill Hickok. It helped popularize the myth that Hickok and Calamity Jane were romantically involved. The theme was picked up and expanded in a series by movie westerns, which in many ways drew on the traditions of the dime novel.

The supposed romantic tie between these two western legends was so popular with the public that it inspired a bizarre hoax. In 1941, a woman named Jean Hickok McCormick appeared on a radio program and claimed that she was the daughter of Wild Bill Hickok and Calamity Jane. She said she had diaries, written in the form of letters to McCormick, that Jane had kept during her years in the American West. According to the diaries, Bill and Jane had married at a camp on the Kansas prairie in 1871, five years before they had actually met. The couple, according to McCormick's story, never lived together, and Hickok told no one of the marriage for fear that one of his many enemies would try to hurt his wife and their infant daughter. McCormick claimed that they eventually divorced, and she was adopted by a sea captain who took her to live in England. There, her mother visited her twice while performing with Buffalo Bill's Wild West.

The story received national attention. The public seemed eager to believe McCormick's romantic and sad tale of Wild Bill and Calamity Jane's thwarted love. McCormick even persuaded the U.S. government to give her a pension because of Hickok's military service.

In the 1950s, experts examined the diaries and declared them fakes. The evaluation could not have been too difficult. The diaries were written in beautiful handwriting that looked much like McCormick's own. It was fairly obvious that McCormick was much more likely the author than Calamity Jane, who probably could not read or write. Even after McCormick's fraud had been exposed, however, biographers and filmmakers continued to use her diaries as a source. As recently as 1995, the television movie *Buffalo Girls* drew on information invented by McCormick.

REEXAMINING THE WEST

Despite the popular appeal of legendary western characters, by the mid-twentieth century historians of the American West began to reexamine these figures in an effort to separate fact from fiction. The most prominent modern biographer of Wild Bill Hickok is Joseph G. Rosa. Starting with *They Called Him Wild Bill* (1964), he wrote a series of books that meticulously examined the available historical records about Hickok. Rosa's work helped disprove many of the more fanciful claims about Hickok's life.

During the same period, the popularity of movie westerns featuring Wild Bill Hickok and other heroic Westerners had begun to fade. Especially after World War II (1939–1945), many people became less intrigued by traditional westerns, with their all-good heroes and all-bad villains. Instead, they became interested in more complicated characters and a more complex view of the American past.

Like many of the most popular westerns of recent years, the best modern film depictions of Wild Bill Hickok treat the character less as a legendary hero and more as a real person dealing imperfectly with the pressures of his mythical reputation. The film *Wild Bill* (1995), largely based on the novel *Deadwood* (1986) by Pete Dexter, deals with the last days of Hickok as he struggles to come to terms with his life and his legend. The television series *Deadwood* (2004–2006), at the beginning of its first season, similarly depicted a somber Hickok living out his final weeks. Neither production, however, could resist

Wild Bill on Film

Almost as soon as movies were invented, Wild Bill Hickok was a character in them. The character first appeared in a 1915 silent movie titled *In the Days of '75 and '76, or The Thrilling Lives of Wild Bill and Calamity Jane.* Filmed on location in South Dakota and Nebraska, it portrayed the two western legends as a married couple. More widely seen was the 1923 silent film *Wild Bill Hickok.* It starred William S. Hart, who became famous playing cowboys. The movie focused on a romantic triangle between Calamity Jane, Hickok, and a woman from the East.

After having supporting roles in a series of westerns, the character of Hickok was again front and center in *The Plainsman* (1936). This big-budget production featured stars Gary Cooper as Hickok and Jean Arthur as Calamity Jane. Based on Frank J. Wilstach's fanciful 1926 biography of Hickok, the movie infuriated Hickok's living relatives. As they had with the earlier Hickok films, they objected to the Wild Bill character's involvement with Calamity Jane, who in real life had been an alcoholic and a prostitute. Howard L. Hickok, Wild Bill's nephew, wrote an angry letter to the film's director, Cecil B. DeMille: "Imagine how our family felt, the uncle whose memory we loved and revered, portrayed on the nation's screen as the lover of Calamity Jane . . . (whose shortcomings had been known to us for years)." DeMille and screenwriter Jean MacPherson had decided not to marry the two

suggesting at least a hint of romantic connection between Wild Bill and Calamity Jane. In *Wild Bill,* the pair are lovers, while in *Deadwood,* Hickok tries to ignore the adoring glances of a lovelorn Jane.

A LIVING LEGEND

Although much has changed about the way Wild Bill Hickok has been presented in print and on film, the public fascination for him has never died. This continuing interest was clear during a 2003 characters, but instead to give them a love-hate relationship. A great success, *The Plainsman* inspired a string of movies in the 1940s in which Wild Bill Hickok was played by Bill Elliot. The actor became so closely associated with the role that he was eventually billed as Wild Bill Elliot.

The most noteworthy appearance of Hickok in the films of the 1950s was in *Calamity Jane*. This time, the romance between Jane and Bill was set to music. The musical starred popular singer Doris Day and Broadway star Howard Keel as the fabled lovers. During the 1950s, Hickok also made the transition to television. *The Adventures of Wild Bill Hickok* ran for seven years and was nominated for an Emmy Award for Best Western or Adventure Series (1955).

In the late twentieth century, traditional western films went out of fashion. But Hickok did make occasional appearances in a new type of western that explored both the reality of life in the American West and the effect that western myths had on the nation and its people. Such films included *Little Big Man* (1970) and *Wild Bill* (1995). The most recent examination of Hickok on film was the television series *Deadwood* (2004–2006). Although the series's producers and creators took pains to depict the harsh, rough world of the remote mining town, they still followed the long Hollywood tradition of romanticizing Wild Bill. Portrayed by Keith Carradine, *Deadwood*'s Hickok is far more decent and noble a man than the real Bill was in his sad final days.

auction of memorabilia from the estate of Hickok's sister Celinda, held in San Francisco. The jewel of the collection was a love letter written by Hickok to his wife dated June 2, 1876, two months before he died. On stationery from the Metropolitan Hotel in Omaha, Nebraska, it read:

> Doll one word from Omaha I was very sick all last night but am feeling very well and happy now god Bless and Protect my Agnes is my Prair [prayer] would I not like

to Put my big hands on your Sholdiers and kiss you rite now Love to emma [Agnes's daughter from a previous marriage] one Thousand Kises to my wife Agnes From your ever loving Husband J B Hickok Wild Bill By By.

The winning bidder purchased the letter at an unexpectedly high price of $190,400, a bid that set a world record.

For those with less cash, a trip to Troy Grove, Illinois, is a far less expensive way of connecting with Hickok and his world. Hickok's birthplace there was a tourist attraction until it was torn down in 1929. A state park now stands on the old Hickok family homestead. The park features a granite monument and a large bust of Hickok carved from a log.

Just seven miles (11.2 kilometers) away, in the nearby town of Mendota, Hickok is honored with a life-size bronze sculpture on the grounds of the Mendota Museum & Historical Society. Dedicated in 2008, the sculpture is based on a photograph taken of Hickok during his one visit to Mendota in 1869.

For Hickok enthusiasts, the most popular tourist destination is Deadwood, South Dakota. After the Black Hills gold rush ended, the town experienced some hard times. Throughout much of the twentieth century, its population shrank as its economy faltered. In 1989, however, Deadwood's fortunes changed when South Dakota legalized gambling there. Both its dozens of casinos and its historic past now draw thousands of visitors to the town each year.

Throughout Deadwood, billboards and signs for restaurants and casinos are plastered with images of its most famous resident. Even though Wild Bill Hickok lived in the town for only a few weeks, he is now forever associated with the place where he met his violent end. In fact, during the tourist season, one of Deadwood's greatest attractions is a daily recreation of his murder.

Every day in the summer, an actor playing Hickok arrives at the No. 10 Saloon ready for an afternoon of poker playing. The scene always ends the same way—with a gunshot to the back of his head. In real life, a single bullet from Jack McCall's gun laid low Wild Bill

Hickok and other Wild West legends continue to be popular, thanks to movies, books, and TV shows based on their lives. In Deadwood, South Dakota, tourists can watch a reenactment of Hickok's fateful poker game, view a replica of the chair in which he was shot, and visit his and Calamity Jane's gravesites. Pictured is the Wild Bill Bar, which sits on the site of the original No. 10 Saloon.

Hickok for all time. In the fantasy staged in Deadwood, however, Hickok is killed each day, only to rise up and return to the poker table the next. In this way, the Deadwood production mirrors the legend of Wild Bill Hickok. More than 130 years after the death of James Butler Hickok, the mythic Wild Bill remains alive and well, always ready to live another day.

CHRONOLOGY

1837   James Butler Hickok is born in Homer (Troy Grove), Illinois, on May 27.

1856   Leaves Illinois for Kansas with his brother Lorenzo.

1858   Is elected constable of Monticello Township in Kansas; is hired by Russell, Majors, and Waddell as a teamster.

1861   Kills David McCanles at Rock Creek Station.

1861–1865   Works as a wagon master, scout, and possibly a spy for the Union Army during the Civil War; is first called by the name "Wild Bill Hickok."

1865   Kills Davis Tutt in a shootout in Springfield, Missouri; meets journalist George Ward Nichols.

1867   Joins the Hancock campaign in the Plains Indian War; becomes a national celebrity with the publication of Nichols's article in *Harper's New Monthly Magazine;* meets journalist Henry M. Stanley; appointed deputy U.S. marshal.

1869   Is elected sheriff of Ellis County, Kansas; kills Bill Mulrey and Samuel Strawhun in two separate incidents; loses reelection bid.

1870   Kills one soldier and wounds another in a bar-room brawl in Hays City.

1871   Becomes the marshal of Abilene, Kansas; meets Agnes Lake Thatcher; kills Phil Coe in a street fight; is dismissed from his position as Abilene's marshal.

1872   Appears in the "Great Buffalo Hunt" at Niagara Falls.

1873   Writes to newspapers to debunk the rumors that he has been killed; joins a show organized by William F. "Buffalo Bill" Cody.

TIMELINE

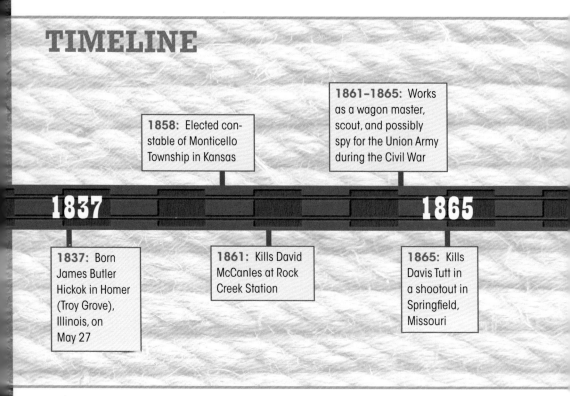

1858: Elected constable of Monticello Township in Kansas

1861–1865: Works as a wagon master, scout, and possibly spy for the Union Army during the Civil War

1837   1865

1837: Born James Butler Hickok in Homer (Troy Grove), Illinois, on May 27

1861: Kills David McCanles at Rock Creek Station

1865: Kills Davis Tutt in a shootout in Springfield, Missouri

1874   Quits show business; returns to the West.

1876   Marries Agnes Lake Thatcher in Cheyenne, Wyoming Territory, and honeymoons in St. Louis, Missouri, and Cincinnati, Ohio; attempts unsuccessfully to lead an expedition to the gold fields of the Black Hills; travels with friend Charlie Utter from Cheyenne to Deadwood, meeting Calamity Jane on the way; is murdered by Jack McCall in Nuttall & Mann's No. 10 Saloon on August 2 and buried in Deadwood.

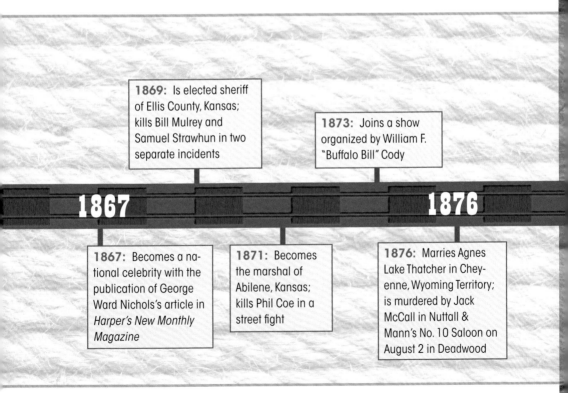

1869: Is elected sheriff of Ellis County, Kansas; kills Bill Mulrey and Samuel Strawhun in two separate incidents

1873: Joins a show organized by William F. "Buffalo Bill" Cody

1867

1876

1867: Becomes a national celebrity with the publication of George Ward Nichols's article in *Harper's New Monthly Magazine*

1871: Becomes the marshal of Abilene, Kansas; kills Phil Coe in a street fight

1876: Marries Agnes Lake Thatcher in Cheyenne, Wyoming Territory; is murdered by Jack McCall in Nuttall & Mann's No. 10 Saloon on August 2 in Deadwood

GLOSSARY

abolitionist   A person opposed to the practice of slavery.

Civil War   Conflict lasting from 1861 to 1865 that pitted southern states seeking to start their own country (the Confederacy) against northern states that remained loyal to the United States (the Union).

Confederacy   Southern states that seceded from and fought against the Union during the Civil War.

constable   A law officer with limited authority, usually working in a small town.

cow town   A town heavily involved in the cattle trade.

desperado   A criminal.

dime novels   Cheaply produced adventure novels that were popular with American readers in the late nineteenth century.

engraving   An illustration printed using a metal plate on which the picture is carved.

frontier   An area that borders an unsettled wilderness.

Great Plains   A dry, flat region in the central United States that was once home to herds of wild buffalo.

marshal   A law officer, usually elected or appointed by a town or city government.

Plains Indian Wars   A series of conflicts during the late nineteenth century between the U.S. Army and various Indian groups of the Great Plains.

reservation   An area of land set aside for the exclusive use of one or more American Indian groups.

saloon   A business in which alcoholic beverages are sold and consumed.

scout   A person sent ahead of a military force to gather information about the enemy.

teamster   A driver of a team of animals that pulls a wagon or coach.

territory   A defined area within the United States that is not yet, but may become, a state.

Underground Railroad   Network of safe houses established in the nineteenth century to help fugitive slaves escape to freedom in the northern United States or Canada.

Union   Northern states that remained loyal to the United States and fought against the Confederacy during the Civil War.

western   A movie or television show set in the American West during the late nineteenth century.

Wild West show   An outdoor show popular in the late nineteenth century that featured famous western figures and cowboy and Indian performers.

BIBLIOGRAPHY

Ames, John. *The Real Deadwood: True Life Histories of Wild Bill Hickok, Calamity Jane, Outlaw Towns, and Other Characters of the Lawless West.* New York: Chamberlain Bros., 2004.

Lamar, Howard R., ed. *The New Encyclopedia of the American West.* New Haven, Conn.: Yale University Press, 1998.

Legends of America. "Old West Legends: Wild Bill—1867 Harper's Weekly Article." Available online at *http://www.legendsof america.com/WE-WildBill.html.*

McLaird, James D. *Wild Bill Hickok & Calamity Jane: Deadwood Legends.* Pierre: South Dakota State Historical Society Press, 2008.

Milner, Clyde A. II, Carol A. O'Connor, and Martha A. Sandweiss, eds. *The Oxford History of the American West.* New York: Oxford University Press, 1994.

Rosa, Joseph G. *They Called Him Wild Bill.* 2nd ed. Norman: University of Oklahoma Press, 1974.

———. *The West of Wild Bill Hickok.* Norman: University of Oklahoma Press, 1982.

———. *Wild Bill Hickok: Gunfighter.* Norman: University of Oklahoma Press, 2003.

———. *Wild Bill Hickok: The Man and His Myth.* Lawrence: University Press of Kansas, 1996.

FURTHER RESOURCES

Books

Cox, J. Randolph, ed. *Dashing Diamond Dick and Other Classic Dime Novels*. New York: Penguin Classics, 2007.

Faber, Doris. *Calamity Jane: Her Life and Her Legend*. Boston: Houghton Mifflin, 1992.

Green, Carl R., and William R. Sanford. *Wild Bill Hickok*. Rev. ed. Berkeley Heights, N.J.: Enslow Publishers, 2008.

Pechan, Bev, and Bill Groethe. *Deadwood: 1876–1976*. Mount Pleasant, S.C.: Arcadia Publishing, 2005.

Phillips, Larissa. *Wild Bill Hickok: Legend of the Wild West*. New York: Rosen Publishing, 2004.

Sonneborn, Liz. *The American West: An Illustrated History*. New York: Scholastic, 2002.

Films

Calamity Jane, DVD. Directed by David Butler. 1953, Burbank, Calif.: Warner Home Video, 2005.

The Plainsman, DVD. Directed by Cecil B. DeMille. 1936, Universal City, Calif.: Universal Studios Home Entertainment, 2004.

Web Sites

The Adams Museum and House

http://www.adamsmuseumandhouse.org/adamscharacters.php
This museum site features brief biographies and photographs of Wild Bill Hickok, Calamity Jane, Charlie Utter, Jack McCall,

and other prominent figures in the early history of Deadwood, South Dakota.

American Experience: Buffalo Bill

http://www.pbs.org/wgbh/americanexperience/cody
On this Web site, the Public Broadcasting Service (PBS) offers its documentary film about the life and legend of William F. "Buffalo Bill" Cody, which was broadcast as part of PBS's American Experience series.

American Treasures of the Library of Congress: Dime Novels

http://www.loc.gov/exhibits/treasures/tri015.html
This page of the Library of Congress's Web site displays the covers of a selection of dime novels in its collection.

City of Deadwood

http://www.cityofdeadwood.com
The official site of the modern city of Deadwood, South Dakota, includes essays about its unique history and about the Mount Moriah Cemetery, in which Wild Bill Hickok is buried.

Legends of America, "Old West Legends: Wild Bill—1867 *Harper's Weekly* Article"

http://www.legendsofamerica.com/WE-WildBill.html
This site reproduces that text of George Ward Nichols's famous profile of Wild Bill Hickok, which appeared in the February 1867 issue of *Harper's New Monthly Magazine*.

Topics in Kansas History: Old West

http://www.kshs.org/research/topics/oldwest/essay.htm
This online essay provided by the Kansas State Historical Society explores Kansas's role in the late nineteenth century cattle trade and touches on Wild Bill Hickok's tenure as a lawman in Hays City and Abilene.

Wild Bill's Last Trail

http://www.gutenberg.org/files/21113/21113-h/21113-h.htm
Project Gutenberg offers the complete text of *Wild Bill's Last Trail* (1904), a dime novel written by Ned Buntline.

PICTURE CREDITS

Page

INDEX

ABOUT THE AUTHOR

Liz Sonneborn is a freelance writer who has long lived in Brooklyn, New York. A graduate of Swarthmore College, she is the author of more than 70 books for children and adults. Sonneborn has written extensively about the history of the western United States. Her books include *The American West: An Illustrated History*, *The California Gold Rush*, *The Mormon Trail*, *Women of the American West*, *Chronology of American Indian History*, and *A to Z of American Indian Women*.